Practical Strategies for Managing Symptoms, Embracing Well-Being, Achieving Long-Term Holistic Health

OVERCOMING ANXIETY *and* DEPRESSION

LILLYIN LOVE

Copyright © 2024

LiL'Love Publications LLC lillovepublishing.com lilly@lillovepublishing.com

Publisher's Cataloging-in-Publication data

Names: Love, Lillyin, author.

Title: Overcoming Anxiety and Depression: Practical Strategies for Managing Symptoms, Embracing Well-Being, Achieving Long-Term Holistic Health / by Lillyin Love.

Description: Includes bibliographical references. | Los Angeles, CA. LiL'Love Publications, 2024.

Library of Congress Control Number: LCCN: 2023918734

|ISBN: 979-8-9892362-2-0 (hardcover) |ISBN: 979-8-9892362-0-6 (Paperback) |ISBN: 979-8-9892362-1-3 (ebook)

Subjects: LCSH Anxiety. | Anxiety--Treatment. | Depression. | Depression-Treatment. | Mental health. | Self-help. | BISAC HEALTH & FITNESS / Mental Health | SELF-HELP / Anxieties & Phobias | SELF-HELP / Mood Disorders / Depression

Classification: LCC RC537. L68 2023| DDC 616.852-dc23 LC record at https://lccn.gov/2023918734

Richard Weber Cover photo of Lilly at Elfin Cove Hot Springs, Alaska./Illustrations by Lillyin Love/Cover Design by Hennah 99designs/Yoga Poses by Mia D Fiverr/Kellee Raymond Back Cover photo/Editing Fiona Grace

To my father, Jack Raymond, my favorite writer.

But really,

for you and me together, dear reader, as our guide on our holistic journey of embracing mind-body and spirit.

To my father, Jack Raymond, my favorite writer.

But really,

**for you and me together, dear reader, as our guide on our holistic
journey of embracing mind-body and spirit.**

CONTENTS

FOREWORD

LORIN LINDNER, PHD, MPH
LOCKWOOD ANIMAL RESCUE CENTER
SERENITY PARK SANCTUARY CEO AND
PRESIDENT

HUMAN EMOTIONS ARE OFTEN fraught with complexity and our busy lives invariably leave us with little time for introspection and self-care. According to current estimates, anxiety and depression are considered the "common cold" of mental health and affect a good proportion of the population at any one time. Therefore, at some point in our lives, many of us will face these formidable emotional adversaries, yet there are well-researched methods that have been shown to provide a positive antidote to despair.

It is with great pleasure for me to introduce to you "Overcoming Anxiety and Depression: Practical Strategies for Managing Symptoms, Embracing Well-Being, Achieving Long-Term Holistic Health" by Lillyin Love. As the title clearly states, this is a practical step-by-step guide by which you can relieve symptoms of both anxiety and depression through natural holistic practices. And with no side effects! Lilly is careful to explain throughout

that this book is not a substitute for professional care from a licensed clini-
tion, but a naturally based supplement and addition to such treatment. As
a practicing psychologist, since 1988 I have come to see that many roads
lead to Rome and that there is no one "best path" to take. In fact, many
effective paths have been neglected by the mental health profession. That
is why it is with great pleasure and pride that I have been able to witness
the wondrous journey of growth by Lilly and how, through incorporating
many of these holistic practices into her own life, she has come to write this
illuminating book.

I started working with Lilly in 2005 at Serenity Park Sanctuary, a tranquil
oasis located on the grounds of the Greater Los Angeles Veterans Administration Healthcare Center in West Los Angeles, CA. At this inno-
vative program where parrots are part of the healing process, veterans with
Post-traumatic Stress Disorder (PTSD) came to seek help outside of the
brick and mortar of the typical hospital setting. Here Lilly began her own
profound personal journey, and this has shaped her compassion, empathy,
and knowledge-base. Now, through her book, Lilly guides you through
these natural and transformative remedies using both ancient and modern
holistic wisdom.

First, the exploration begins with a deep dive into the multifaceted nature
of anxiety and depression, unraveling the complex interplay of emotions
and thoughts that shape our inner worlds. Through such easily mastered
exercises such as understanding the vagus nerve and the vital importance
of mindful breath work, Lilly uncovers the profound connection between
our physical and mental well-being, thus paving the way for inner peace
and calm. Next, Lilly traverses the terrain of mindfulness and Cognitive-Behavioral Therapy, which helps us cultivate a deeper understanding
of our own inner workings, illuminating the shadows that often obscure

our path to healing. The chapters dedicated to nourishing our mind, body, and spirit through food, exercise, and holistic practices, such as yoga, massage, and acupuncture, serve as poignant reminders of the innate healing potential that resides within us.

Utilizing a wide spectrum of healing modalities, Lilly reminds us of the intrinsic value of restorative practices such as sleep, affirmations, and visualizations, which hold the power to transform negative thought patterns and ignite the flame of positivity and creativity within us. Further, Lilly points out the significance of social connections and the art of relaxation, which can serve as guiding lights on our journey towards self-compassion and serenity, instilling in us a renewed sense of resilience and fortitude.

As we arrive at the epilogue of this restorative odyssey, we are filled with a sense of hope and empowerment, knowing that the landscape of mental health is not a bleak expanse but a realm brimming with the potential for growth and transformation.

During nearly 40 years of working with hundreds of patients, I can wholeheartedly support the holistic practices found in this book, whether as a supplement to professional psychotherapy or as stand-alone remedies for many. I extend to you an invitation to embark on this enlightening voyage of self-discovery and healing, where the keys to overcoming anxiety and depression await to open the door to a more contented inner world. I applaud Lilly's dedication and courage to bring the light of natural holistic practices to the darkness of anxiety and depression.

Lorin Lindner, PhD, MPH (she/hers) Lockwood Animal Rescue Center (LARC) Serenity Park Sanctuary CEO and President www.lockwooda rc.org http://www.instagram.com/lockwoodanimalrescuecenter/ May 5, 2024

INTRODUCTION

BREAKING FREE FROM THE PRISON OF ANXIETY AND DEPRESSION

Just when the caterpillar thought the world was over,
it became a butterfly. -Proverb

I FERVENTLY BELIEVE THAT anxiety and depression do not define you. Anxiety and depression trick us into thinking we're just a caterpillar. You and I know that's merely a part of our story. The truth is you can rewrite the caterpillar chapter with courage and determination. We can use the tools and strategies presented in this book. We have the opportunity to reclaim our lives, discover our inner strength, and thrive beyond anxiety's shadow and depression's grip. This book will help unfurl our wings, and we will become the butterflies we were always meant to be.

Remember, you are not alone on this journey. Alongside you are countless individuals who have faced depression and conquered anxiety, emerging on the other side with newfound freedom and resilience.

Let their stories and shared experiences inspire you and remind you that profound change is possible.

While anxiety and depression are distinct mental health conditions, many therapy approaches can effectively treat both disorders. This is because there are common underlying mechanisms and cognitive patterns that contribute to both anxiety and depression. In this book, we will be learning ways in which therapies and exercises can address symptoms of both anxiety and depression.

In this fast-paced, high-pressure modern world, anxiety has become an all-too-familiar companion for many of us, as well as the veil of depression's hold on us, which can be suffocating, affecting our thoughts, emotions, and actions, and leaving us feeling trapped in a never-ending cycle of worry and fear. This book is a guiding light, offering comfort, understanding, and practical tools to break free from the prison of anxiety and depression.

Anxiety is a complex and multifaceted phenomenon that affects millions of people worldwide. From the occasional twinge of nervousness before a big presentation to the debilitating panic attacks that strike seemingly out of nowhere, anxiety can range from mild to severe, transient to chronic. It can manifest in various forms, such as generalized anxiety disorder, social anxiety, phobias, and post-traumatic stress disorder, among others.

Depression is another common mental health disorder that can significantly impact a person's well-being and social connections. It is characterized by persistent feelings of sadness, hopelessness, and a lack of interest or pleasure in activities. Depression can range from mild to severe and can last for short periods or become chronic.

Depression can have a profound effect on social connections, causing individuals to withdraw from social interactions. They may isolate themselves, avoid social events, and have difficulty connecting with others emotionally. Depression can contribute to a sense of loneliness and a feeling of being disconnected from others.

One of the key symptoms of depression is a negative perception of self, leading to low self-esteem and self-worth. Individuals with depression often have difficulty believing that others would genuinely want to engage with them or be interested in their company. These negative beliefs about themselves can create barriers to forming and maintaining social connections.

Depression can also affect communication and interpersonal skills. Individuals may have trouble expressing themselves, articulating their emotions, or engaging in conversations. They may feel a lack of motivation or energy, making social interactions feel exhausting or overwhelming.

Additionally, depression can impact a person's ability to perceive social cues accurately. They may interpret neutral or positive interactions as hostile or dismissive, leading to miscommunication or strained relationships. This distorted perception can further contribute to social withdrawal and isolation.

It is not uncommon for individuals to experience both depression and anxiety together. These conditions can often feed into one another, with anxiety exacerbating depressive symptoms and vice versa.

Seeking professional help from a mental health practitioner is crucial for individuals struggling with depression and anxiety. Treatment options such as therapy, medication, or a combination of both can help individuals address these conditions, alleviate symptoms, and improve overall social well-being.

But this book is not just about theory and knowledge. It is a practical guide filled with evidence-based strategies, techniques, and exercises that have been proven effective in managing depression and reducing anxiety. You will be introduced to the vagus nerve and its interplay with anxiety, mindfulness practices, cognitive-behavioral techniques, relaxation exercises, and self-care rituals that can help you take control of your anxious thoughts and depressed emotions. You will also discover the power of self-compassion, resilience, and finding meaning in adversity, which are essential ingredients in the journey toward freedom from anxiety. I have included valuable self-guided meditations, visualizations, and affirmations to help soothe the soul and help break depression's iron grip.

Throughout these pages, I recognize that overcoming anxiety or depression is not a linear path or a destination with a fixed endpoint. It is a dynamic process that requires patience, persistence, and the willingness to face discomfort and uncertainty. I invite you to embark on this transformative journey armed with knowledge, compassion, and a commitment to self-growth.

All the world is full of suffering, it is also full of overcoming. -Helen Keller

So, take a deep breath, open your heart and mind, and let this book be your guiding light toward a life liberated from the chains of anxiety and the jail cell of depression. May it serve as a beacon of hope, leading you toward a future filled with peace, joy, and limitless possibilities.

Prepare to embark on a transformative journey. -Lillyin Love

Chapter One

Navigating the Landscape of Anxiety and Depression

Our Journey Begins

Action is the antidote to anxiety. -Peter Zarlenga

BRAVE TRAVELER, WELCOME TO the first chapter of our voyage through the enchanting world of anxiety management and depression relief. In this chapter, we shall embark on a bold exploration of the intricate landscapes of symptoms, delving deep into their roots, understanding their many manifestations, and uncovering the hidden pathways to tranquility. With a fearless heart and an unwavering commitment to peace, let us navigate the twists and turns of this challenging terrain, **illuminating the path to a calmer, more centered existence.**

Anxiety, that relentless companion that often shadows our every step, is not an enemy to be vanquished but rather a messenger, offering us valuable insights into the deepest recesses of our being. Like a flickering flame, it can either consume us in its fiery embrace or ignite within us a newfound resilience and strength. By unraveling the mysteries of **anxiety** and embracing the lessons learned from **depression**, we transcend their power and emerge as victors, reclaiming our inner calm and serenity. We can overcome fear and emerge more assertive with a resilience that will carry over to all aspects of our lives.

Manifestations of Anxiety:

Anxiety is a shape-shifting entity, assuming many guises as it weaves through the fabric of our lives. From the gentle ripples of worry to the tumultuous waves of panic, **anxiety manifests** in myriad forms, each with its unique set of challenges. Some common **manifestations of anxiety** include:

1. Generalized Anxiety: This persistent and excessive worry about everyday events and activities can dominate our thoughts, leaving us trapped in an unrelenting cycle of unease.

2. Social Anxiety: A fear of judgment and rejection in social situations can make even the most straightforward interactions feel like walking on a tightrope, leading to avoidance and isolation.

3. Panic Attacks: These sudden and intense episodes of fear can strike without warning, overwhelming us with a barrage of physical and psychological symptoms, often leaving us feeling helpless and out of control.

4. Phobias: Specific fears or aversions, such as fear of heights or spiders, can cause extreme anxiety and interfere with our daily lives, restricting our movements and activities

5. Obsessive-Compulsive Disorder (OCD): Intrusive and persistent thoughts, often accompanied by compulsive behaviors, can consume our thoughts and hinder our ability to function.

6. Post-Traumatic Stress Disorder (PTSD): Anxiety triggered by past traumatic experiences can haunt us, making it difficult to move forward and find peace in the present.

Depression's Deceptions:

Depression can manifest in various ways and can affect individuals differently. Here are some common manifestations of depression:

1. Persistent sadness or low mood: One of the central features of depression is experiencing a prolonged feeling of sadness, emptiness, or hopelessness. This sadness may be present throughout the day and most days of the week.

2. Loss of interest or pleasure: Depression often leads to a loss of interest or pleasure in once-enjoyable activities. Hobbies, social interactions, and even basic self-care routines may become mundane or unappealing.

3. Fatigue and lack of energy: Individuals with depression often report feeling tired, physically drained, and lacking energy even after minimal exertion. This may result in decreased productivity and difficulty completing daily tasks.

4. Changes in appetite and weight: Depression can impact appetite, leading to changes in eating habits. Some individuals may experience a loss of appetite and weight loss, while others may have an increased appetite and weight gain.

5. Sleep disturbances: Depression can disrupt sleep patterns, leading to insomnia (difficulty falling asleep or staying asleep) or hypersomnia (excessive sleepiness during the day and prolonged hours of sleep).

6. Difficulty concentrating and making decisions: Depressive symptoms can make it challenging to focus, make decisions, or remember important information. This can affect work or school performance and lead to feelings of frustration and self-doubt.

7. Feelings of worthlessness or guilt: Individuals with depression often have negative thoughts about themselves, feeling a sense of worthlessness or excessive guilt. They may have an exaggerated focus on past mistakes and blame themselves for things that are beyond their control.

8. Withdrawal from social activities: Depression can lead to social withdrawal and a loss of interest in engaging with others. Individuals may isolate themselves, avoid social interaction, and prefer spending time alone.

9. Physical symptoms: Depression can also manifest as physical symptoms such as headaches, back pain, digestive problems, or unexplained aches and pains.

10. Suicidal thoughts: In severe cases, depression can lead to thoughts of death or suicide. If you or someone you know is experiencing suicidal thoughts, **it is imperative to seek immediate professional**

help. It's essential to remember that everyone's experience of depression can differ, and not everyone will exhibit all of these symptoms.

Cultivating the Path to Calm:

This book is not meant to replace the medical profession in the treatment of anxiety or depression when necessary but to supplement and reduce symptoms with easy and quick remedies that can be done by anyone suffering. These remedies will work on any anxiety, no matter how long or short the duration. They will also help alleviate depression in its myriad of forms.

Now that we have explored the diverse manifestations of various symptoms. Let us illuminate the path to serenity, drawing upon ancient wisdom and modern insights to guide us through their treacherous terrain. By cultivating a repertoire of stress-management techniques and fostering a mindset of resilience and self-compassion, we can forge a path toward a calmer, more centered existence.

1. Grounding Techniques: When anxiety threatens to sweep us off our feet, grounding techniques anchor us in the present moment, providing stability and solace. Simple practices such as deep belly breathing, engaging our senses, or using a mantra can redirect our attention away from anxious thoughts, grounding us in the here and now. Sometimes, the mere act of holding onto a chair's armrest or planting your feet firmly on the ground can reset and re-send a more calming, reassuring message to the brain.

2. Cognitive Restructuring: Depression and anxiety often stem from distorted thinking patterns, magnifying our fears and limiting our perspective. Cognitive restructuring involves identifying and challenging these unhelpful thoughts and replacing them with more balanced and realistic beliefs. By reframing our thoughts, we can unlock doors to new possibilities and release the grip of anxiety and depression.

3. Exposure Therapy: Facing our fears head-on may seem daunting, but exposure therapy offers a powerful opportunity for growth and liberation. Gradually and safely confronting anxiety-provoking situations or triggers, we desensitize ourselves to their power, reclaiming control over our lives and diminishing anxiety's hold.

4. Self-Compassion and Acceptance: Amidst the tumult of anxiety, self-compassion becomes a vital lifeline, offering comfort and support. By acknowledging and **accepting our emotions without judgment,** we foster a kind and gentle relationship with ourselves. By embracing imperfections and **treating ourselves with loving kindness**, we create a sanctuary of acceptance where depression's power is gently diminished, and anxiety fades away.

5. Lifestyle Changes: We take a holistic approach to health management and recognize the crucial role lifestyle factors play in our emotional well-being. Incorporating regular exercise, a balanced diet, restful sleep, and nurturing self-care practices into our lives fortifies our resilience and creates a solid foundation for peace and calm.

As we navigate the intricacies of a symptomatic landscape, we must remember that the path to tranquility is not a smooth and straight road. It is a winding and meandering journey, filled with setbacks and triumphs, but ultimately leading us toward a life infused with inner calm and resilience. With these foundational insights and transformative techniques as our compass, we venture forth fearlessly, reclaiming serenity and joy in the face of anxiety's tempestuous storms and depressions' deepest, darkest valleys. Embrace this chapter as a guide on your voyage, infused with the richness of understanding and the promise of a brighter horizon. May you continue to navigate the path with courage and grace, knowing that tranquility and peace await you just beyond the next page. You will learn of the magic vagus nerve in managing anxiety and depression.

CHAPTER TWO

THE VAGUS NERVE MAGIC IN OUR BODIES

THE CONNECTION TO OUR BODIES

Anxiety is like a rocking chair. It gives you something to do, but it doesn't get you very far. -Jodi Picoult

HERE, YOU WILL FIND a simple explanation of the vagus nerve and exercises that anyone can do to activate it for stress management.

The vagus nerve is the longest cranial nerve in the body. It starts in the brainstem, travels down the neck, and branches out into various organs in the chest and abdomen. The vagus nerve is a key player in the parasympathetic nervous system, which is responsible for regulating the body's rest and relaxation response.

When the vagus nerve is activated, it promotes a sense of calm and relaxation. It helps reduce the effects of stress and anxiety by slowing down your heart rate, lowering blood pressure, and reducing inflammation in the body. By activating the vagus nerve, you can effectively manage anxiety and stress levels.

Simple Exercises to Activate the Vagus Nerve:

1. Deep diaphragmatic breathing: Find a comfortable position, either sitting or lying down. Place one hand on your chest and the other on your abdomen. Take a slow, deep breath through your nose, expanding your abdomen and feeling your hand rise. Exhale slowly through your mouth, allowing your abdomen to fall. Repeat this deep breathing pattern for several minutes, focusing on the sensation of relaxation with each breath.

Benefits: Deep breathing stimulates the vagus nerve and activates the relaxation response in the body. It helps decrease anxiety, relax muscles, and lower heart rate.

2. Humming: Close your eyes and take a few deep breaths to relax. Gently press your lips together and make a buzzing sound like a **bee** or hum a low-pitched sound. Feel the vibration in your face and throat as you hum. Continue humming for a few minutes, focusing on the sensation and allowing it to bring a sense of calmness to your body.

Benefits: Humming stimulates the vagus nerve and triggers the release of calming neurotransmitters. It can reduce depression, promote relaxation, and improve overall well-being.

3. Cold water face splash: Fill a bowl with cold water or place ice cubes in a washcloth. Close your eyes and take a few deep breaths to prepare. Dip your face into the freezing water or press the washcloth with ice against your forehead and cheeks. Hold it for a few seconds before removing it. This sudden temperature change can stimulate the vagus nerve and has a calming effect on the body.

Benefits: Cold water face splashes activate the vagus nerve and help reduce anxiety by triggering the "Mamilian dive reflex." This reflex slows down your heart rate and promotes a sense of relaxation.

4. Self-massage: Start by massaging your neck and shoulders with your fingertips, using gentle circular motions. Gradually move down to your chest, abdomen, and the area just below your rib cage. Apply light pressure and focus on any areas of tension or discomfort. Massage for several minutes, allowing your body to relax and release stress.

Benefits: Self-massage stimulates the vagus nerve and promotes relaxation. It helps release tension in the body, reduces stress, and improves overall well-being.

5. Laughter therapy: Engage in activities that make you laugh, such as watching funny videos, reading humorous books, or spending time with amusing friends. Laughter stimulates the vagus nerve and releases endorphins, which promote relaxation and reduce uncomfortable feelings. Incorporate laughter into your daily routine to improve your vagal tone and boost your mood.

Benefits: Laughter therapy enhances the vagal tone and helps manage emotions. It boosts your mood, reduces stress hormones, and increases feelings of well-being.

Remember, incorporating these exercises into your daily routine can have a cumulative effect on activating the vagus nerve and reducing anxiety.

Be consistent and patient, and learn to observe their positive impact on your overall well-being. By understanding the role of the vagus nerve in our emotional well-being and incorporating exercises, lifestyle changes, and integrative approaches, we can unlock the power of this essential neural pathway to alleviate symptoms and improve our overall holistic health. It's important to remember that each individual's journey toward vagus nerve activation will be unique and may require a combination of approaches. By prioritizing self-care, seeking professional help when needed, and practicing patience and perseverance, we can unleash the power of the vagus nerve and find greater peace in our lives. This book will definitely aid you in understanding how the vagus nerve can be incorporated into practices that will help you achieve your goal of eliminating negative emotional influences in your life.

In conclusion, the vagus nerve plays a vital role in managing anxiety, and the exercises outlined in this chapter can activate it to promote relaxation and reduce stress. However, it is essential to recognize that anxiety management is a multifaceted process that requires a combination of techniques and practices. By incorporating additional strategies such as progressive muscle relaxation, visualization, journaling, fostering a supportive environment, stress management techniques, and seeking professional help, you can enhance the effectiveness of vagus nerve activation and improve your overall well-being. Remember, each person's journey is unique, so be patient and compassionate with yourself as you navigate the path toward greater peace and tranquility.

In addition to the vagus nerve exercises mentioned, incorporating mindfulness and meditation practices into your daily routine can have a transformative effect on anxiety management. Mindfulness involves being fully present in the moment and observing thoughts and emotions without judgment. This practice allows us to **cultivate a sense of inner calm and detachment from anxious thoughts.**

MEDITATION OF THE FIVE-SENSES

ONE EXERCISE FOR THE **vagus nerve** that can help bring a sense of calm and focus is called the "**Five Senses Meditation.**" This exercise involves tuning into each of your five senses, one by one, and fully immersing yourself in the present moment. By engaging your senses, you can bring your awareness to the present and cultivate a sense of mindfulness.

To begin the exercise, find a comfortable and quiet space where you can sit undisturbed for a few minutes. Close your eyes and take a few deep breaths to settle into the moment.

Start by focusing on your sense of sight. Gradually open your eyes and allow your gaze to settle softly on an object in your surroundings. Observe the details of the object, its shape, color, and texture. Take your time to fully immerse yourself in the visual experience of the object. Notice any thoughts or judgments that arise and gently bring your attention back to the object.

Next, shift your attention to your sense of hearing. Begin by bringing your awareness to the sounds around you. Listen for both the distant and nearby sounds, whether it's the chirping of birds, the hum of traffic, or the rustling of leaves. Allow each sound to come and go without clinging or resisting. Observe the sounds with an open and non-judgmental mindset.

Now, shift your focus to your sense of touch. Gently scan your body for any sensations or points of contact. Notice the texture of your clothes against your skin, the feeling of your feet on the floor, or the air temperature on your skin. Bring your attention to any areas of tension or tightness in your body and allow them to soften with each breath.

Move on to your sense of smell. Take a moment to notice any aromas or scents in your environment. It could be the scent of flowers, fresh-cut grass, or even the aroma of coffee. Please take a few deep breaths, inhale the scent, and let it fill your awareness.

Lastly, focus on your sense of taste. If you have a drink or a snack nearby, take a moment to fully engage in the act of tasting. Pay attention to the flavors, textures, and sensations as you consume the food or drink. Allow yourself to appreciate each bite or sip, savoring the experience. If there is no snack, just roll your tongue around in your mouth across your teeth and then swallow. Take a moment to bring your attention back to your breath.

Throughout this exercise, the idea is to bring your awareness to each sense and fully experience the present moment without judgment or attachment. By engaging your senses, you can ground yourself in the present and cultivate a state of mindfulness. Take your time with each sense, savoring the experience and allowing yourself to be fully in the moment. This exercise can be practiced for a few minutes or as long as you like, and it can be done anytime, anywhere to bring a sense of calm and presence to your day.

Take a moment to check in; notice any thoughts or sensations in your body. It's important to **check in** after each exercise, but really, it's just practicing strengthening this habit when you're feeling anxious. It's important to note that "**checking in**" is just that; just notice what is going on, no judgments about right or wrong, **just notice that's it**. Now that you know proper "**checking-in,**" do it now....Great! **Conscious, worry-free** "**checking-in**" is the most potent weapon in your arsenal against anxiety.

CHAPTER THREE

BREATH THE SOURCE OF LIFE

TRANSFORMATIVE POWER OF BREATHING TECHNIQUES TO CALM YOUR ANXIETY AND DEPRESSION

When the breath controls your mind, you can control anything. -Swami Rama

WELCOME TO THIS CHAPTER, dedicated to exploring the benefits of breathing exercises in managing and alleviating symptoms. Breathing exercises offer a simple yet powerful technique for calming our minds, relaxing our bodies, and restoring inner tranquility.

Breathing exercises can offer several benefits for individuals experiencing depression. Here are a few ways in which breathing exercises can be helpful:

1. Promotes relaxation: Deep breathing exercises, such as diaphragmatic or belly breathing, activate the body's relaxation response. This triggers the parasympathetic nervous system, reducing feelings of stress, anxiety, and tension.

2. Reduces anxiety: Controlled breathing can help regulate the body's stress response, which is often heightened in individuals with depression. Focusing on slow, deep breaths can help calm an overactive mind and decrease feelings of anxiety.

3. Increases oxygenation: Shallow breathing is common in people with anxiety. Engaging in intentional deep breathing exercises can improve oxygen flow to the brain, enhance mental clarity and cognitive function, and alleviate depression.

4. Mood regulation: Deep breathing exercises can stimulate the vagus nerve, a vital component of the body's relaxation response. This activation can help regulate mood and emotions, potentially reducing depressive symptoms.

5. Redirects focus and interrupts negative thought patterns: Deep breathing exercises encourage individuals to focus on their breath, diverting attention away from negative thoughts and rumination associated with depression.

6. Mind-body connection: Practicing breathing exercises can help individuals better understand their body and emotions. This heightened sensitivity can foster a better understanding of one's internal state and support self-care and self-regulation.

7. Improved sleep: Breathing exercises can assist with relaxation and reduce anxiety, helping individuals achieve a more restful sleep. Better sleep can positively impact overall mood and well-being.

It's important to note that while breathing exercises can be beneficial for managing depressive symptoms, they are not a substitute for professional treatment. It is crucial to seek professional help from a mental health provider for a comprehensive treatment plan.

The Role of Breathing in Anxiety and Depression:

One crucial aspect of anxiety is the connection between our breath and our emotional state. When we experience stress, our breathing tends to become shallow, rapid, and irregular. This shallow breathing disrupts the balance between oxygen and carbon dioxide in our bodies, triggering further physiological stress responses and exacerbating our anxiety symptoms. By **"checking in"** and then learning to regulate our breathing and engage in intentional breathing exercises, we can interrupt this cycle and restore a sense of calm and balance.

Benefits of Breathing Exercises for Anxiety and Depression:

Breathing exercises offer a wide range of benefits for individuals struggling with unwanted emotions. Try different breathing exercises, and then take a moment to **Check-in** with your body/mind connection and notice any difference. Try to notice what your body is feeling and what your associated thoughts are. Try each exercise at least once. This important exercise is where you will notice which ones are easier or more difficult. While you do each breathing exercise, notice your thoughts and sensations in your body. Pay particular attention when experiencing anxiety to notice the before and after with any of the breathwork tools you use. Don't be afraid to make your own version of the breathwork tools. The great thing about using breath as a tool for anxiety management is it's always there, or if not, there's a much bigger issue than anxiety. Relax and play with these breath exercises. There's really no exact right or wrong in the way we breathe. If you're alive, you're doing it right! Focus on your thoughts and sensations in your body and use the breath to unravel the connections to anxiety found there. Notice where the body is tense and learn to **quiet a racing heart with your breath.**

Of course! "Check-in" before and after. Here are five detailed breath exercises for you. Try them all:

Exercise 1: Belly Breathing:

1. FIND A COMFORTABLE SEATED POSITION, EITHER ON A CHAIR OR ON THE FLOOR.

2. PLACE ONE HAND ON YOUR CHEST AND THE OTHER ON YOUR BELLY.

3. TAKE A DEEP BREATH THROUGH YOUR NOSE, ALLOWING YOUR BELLY TO RISE AS YOU FILL YOUR LUNGS WITH AIR.

4. EXHALE SLOWLY THROUGH YOUR MOUTH, FEELING YOUR

BELLY GENTLY SINK BACK TOWARDS YOUR SPINE.

5. CONTINUE TO BREATHE DEEPLY IN THIS MANNER, FO-CUSING ON THE SENSATION OF YOUR BELLY RISING AND FALLING WITH EACH BREATH. AIM FOR A SLOW, STEADY RHYTHM.

CHECK-IN

Exercise 2: Box Breathing:

1. SIT OR STAND COMFORTABLY IN A QUIET SPACE.

2. INHALE SLOWLY AND DEEPLY THROUGH YOUR NOSE TO A COUNT OF FOUR, FEELING YOUR ABDOMEN EXPAND.

3. HOLD YOUR BREATH FOR A COUNT OF FOUR.

4. EXHALE SLOWLY AND COMPLETELY THROUGH YOUR MOUTH TO A COUNT OF FOUR, FEELING YOUR ABDOMEN CONTRACT.

5. HOLD YOUR BREATH AGAIN FOR A COUNT OF FOUR.

6. REPEAT THIS PATTERN FOR SEVERAL ROUNDS, ALLOWING YOURSELF TO SINK INTO A RELAXED STATE WITH EACH BREATH.

CHECK-IN

Exercise 3: 4-7-8 Breath:

1. BEGIN BY SITTING OR LYING DOWN IN A COMFORTABLE POSITION.

2. CLOSE YOUR EYES AND TAKE A DEEP BREATH THROUGH YOUR NOSE TO A COUNT OF FOUR.

3. HOLD YOUR BREATH FOR A COUNT OF SEVEN.

4. SLOWLY EXHALE THROUGH YOUR MOUTH TO A COUNT OF EIGHT, MAKING A WHOOSHING SOUND AS YOU RELEASE THE AIR.

5. REPEAT THIS CYCLE THREE MORE TIMES, FOCUSING ON THE COUNT AND SOUND OF EACH BREATH. GRADUALLY INCREASE THE NUMBER OF REPETITIONS AS YOU BECOME MORE COMFORTABLE WITH THIS EXERCISE.

CHECK-IN

Exercise 4: Equal Breathing:

1. SIT IN A COMFORTABLE POSITION, ENSURING YOUR SPINE IS STRAIGHT AND YOUR SHOULDERS RELAXED.

2. CLOSE YOUR EYES AND BRING YOUR ATTENTION TO YOUR BREATH.

3. INHALE SLOWLY THROUGH YOUR NOSE TO A COUNT OF FOUR.

4. **EXHALE THROUGH YOUR NOSE TO THE SAME COUNT OF FOUR.**

5. **CONTINUE THIS PATTERN OF INHALING AND EXHALING FOR SEVERAL MINUTES, ALLOWING YOUR BREATH TO BECOME SMOOTH AND EVEN.**

CHECK-IN

Exercise 5: Alternate Nostril Breath:

1. **SIT IN A COMFORTABLE POSITION, RESTING YOUR LEFT HAND ON YOUR LEFT KNEE AND BRINGING YOUR RIGHT HAND UP TOWARDS YOUR FACE.**

2. **GENTLY PLACE YOUR RIGHT THUMB ON YOUR RIGHT NOSTRIL, CLOSING IT OFF COMPLETELY.**

3. **INHALE DEEPLY THROUGH YOUR LEFT NOSTRIL.**

4. **PAUSE BRIEFLY, KEEPING BOTH NOSTRILS CLOSED OFF WITH YOUR THUMB AND RING FINGER.**

5. **RELEASE YOUR THUMB AND EXHALE THROUGH YOUR RIGHT NOSTRIL.**

6. **INHALE THROUGH YOUR RIGHT NOSTRIL AND PAUSE BRIEFLY.**

7. **CLOSE OFF YOUR RIGHT NOSTRIL WITH YOUR THUMB AND EXHALE THROUGH YOUR LEFT NOSTRIL.**

8. **CONTINUE THIS CYCLE OF INHALING AND EXHALING THROUGH ALTERNATE NOSTRILS FOR SEVERAL MINUTES, FOCUSING ON THE SENSATION OF THE AIR FLOWING OUT.**

CHECK-IN

Incorporating these exercises into a stress-management practice can lead to the following:

1. **Activation of the relaxation response:** Breathing exercises activate the parasympathetic nervous system, inducing a state of relaxation and countering the "fight-or-flight" response associated with anxiety.

2. **Decreased physiological arousal:** Deep, diaphragmatic breathing can lower our heart rate, reduce muscle tension, and stabilize our blood pressure, promoting overall physical well-being.

3. **Regulation of emotions:** Breathing exercises allow us to regulate our emotions by activating the part of the brain responsible for emotional regulation. This can help us gain control over racing thoughts and overwhelming feelings.

4. **Enhanced self-awareness:** Breathing exercises invite us to develop a deeper connection with our bodies and inner sensations, promoting self-awareness and increasing our understanding of anxiety triggers and patterns.

5. **Improved focus and attention:** By directing our attention to the present moment and our breath, we can cultivate

mindfulness and increase our ability to focus, reducing anxious thoughts and rumination.

Breathing exercises offer a powerful and accessible tool for managing any kind of stress we may be facing. By harnessing the power of our breath, we can restore balance to our minds and bodies, calm our nervous system, and regain a sense of control over chaos. In the following chapters of this book, in addition to breathwork, we will explore techniques and exercises tailored specifically to address symptom manifestations, empowering you in your journey toward emotional well-being and personal growth. Remember, you possess the ability to regulate your breath and find peace and solace within the gentle rhythm of your inhales and exhales. Breathing exercises are an invaluable resource on your path to overcoming depression and embracing a life free of anxiety.

BREATH SOURCE OF LIFE

Breathing in, I smile. Breathing out, I release. Breathing in, I dwell in the present moment. Breathing out, I feel it is a wonderful moment-Thich Nhat Hanh

PREPARE FOR A BREATHTAKING **journey** through five uniquely captivating advanced breathing exercises. Like a blast of pure oxygen filling your lungs, these exercises will transport you to a realm of tranquility and rejuvenation. Each exercise is an artful blend of mindfulness and creativity, designed to invigorate your senses and soothe your soul. So, take a deep breath, let go of any tension, and immerse yourself in this invigorating world of delightful breathing techniques. **Check-in**

THE BLOSSOMING PETAL

IMAGINE YOURSELF AS A DELICATE FLOWER

UNFURLING ITS PETALS IN the warm embrace of the sun. Sit comfortably, spine erect, and place your hands on your belly. As you inhale deeply through your nose, envision your belly expanding like the gentle opening of a flower. Feel the breath nourishing every cell of your being. Now, as you exhale slowly through your mouth, visualize your petals gracefully closing, releasing any tension or worries. With each inhalation and exhalation, witness the blooming and closing of your inner flower, guiding you to a state of inner calm and serenity. Check-in

THE OCEAN'S EMBRACE

IMMERSE IN THE SEA

CLOSE YOUR EYES AND transport yourself to a serene shoreline, where the rhythmic waves caress the sand. Take a moment to observe the ebb and flow of the ocean, mirroring the rise and fall of your breath. Inhale deeply through your nose, imagining you are drawing in the soothing essence of sea air. Let your exhale mimic the gentle retreat of the tide, releasing any stress or tension. As you continue this cycle, allow the imagery of the ocean's embrace to wash away anxiety, leaving you refreshed and grounded, like a seashell nestled in the sand.   Check-in

THE DANCING FLAME

CHANNEL YOUR FIRE

LIGHT A CANDLE AND dim the lights, creating a cozy and intimate atmosphere. Sit in front of the flickering flame, gazing softly into its dance. Inhale deeply through your nose, feeling the warmth and lightness of the flame enter your body. As you exhale through your mouth, imagine your breath fanning the flame, making it dance more vibrantly. With each breath, synchronize your inhalations and exhalations with the flame's graceful movements. Sense the energy and calmness emanating from the flame, harmonizing with your breath, soothing your mind, and kindling a sense of inner peace. Check-in

THE BUTTERFLY WINGS

PICTURE YOURSELF AS A BUTTERFLY

YOU ARE GRACEFULLY FLUTTERING through a vibrant garden. Close your eyes and bring your awareness to your breath. Imagine your wings gently unfurling on each inhalation through your nose, carrying you higher into the sky. Feel the expansion and lightness in your chest as your wings reach their fullest extent. As you exhale through your mouth, envision your wings gracefully folding, drawing you closer to the earth. Repeat this motion, syncing your breath with the butterfly's flight, and feel the sense of liberation and tranquility accompanying each breath. Embrace the freedom and lightness of the butterfly, allowing your worries to fade away with each fluttering breath. Check-in

THE STARRY CONSTELLATION

EXPAND YOUR MIND

FIND A QUIET SPOT under the night sky and lie down, gazing at the stars. Allow yourself to be cradled by the vastness of the universe. Take a deep, cleansing breath in through your nose, and envision yourself inhaling the stars' brilliance. As you exhale through your mouth, imagine exhaling stardust, sending your worries and anxieties into the cosmos. With each inhalation, feel your body infused with celestial energy, expanding your awareness and connection with the universe. Exhale any remaining tension, surrendering it to the infinite beauty surrounding you. Bask in the soothing stillness and cosmic energy, allowing your breath to guide you toward deep relaxation. Check-in

In this breathtaking exploration, you have embarked on a journey through five uniquely enchanting breathing exercises. From the gentle blossoming of a flower to the rhythmic embrace of the ocean, the flickering flame's dance to the graceful flight of a butterfly, and the awe-inspiring vastness of the night sky, each exercise awakens your senses and nurtures your inner peace. So, breathe in the beauty and let these artful techniques infuse your being with tranquility and vitality. Embrace the power of your breath and unlock a world of serenity and renewal. Let your breath be your guide on this remarkable path to inner harmony. Don't Forget To: **Check-in...often.**

CHAPTER FOUR

MINDFULNESS OUR CONNECTION TO OURSELVES

EMBRACE MINDFULNESS FOR RELIEF FROM ANXIETY AND LASTING SERENITY FROM DEPRESSION

The greatest weapon against stress is our ability to choose one thought over another. -William James

I N THIS CHAPTER, WE embark on a transformative journey into the empowering world of mindfulness, where we will uncover its profound ability to manage and alleviate the overwhelming waves of negative emotions that can crash upon our minds.

Mindfulness, a practice rooted in ancient wisdom and now supported by scientific research, offers a practical and accessible way to find peace amidst the chaos of anxious thoughts and emotions. By cultivating a moment-to-moment, non-judgmental awareness of our thoughts, feelings, and bodily sensations, we can forge a resilient fortress, a haven of calmness in the face of life's tumultuous storms.

Understanding Mindfulness:

Imagine mindfulness as a gentle guide, beckoning us to embark on a sacred quest of self-discovery and inner peace. It invites us to pay attention, deliberately and without judgment, to the present moment, like a delicate butterfly settling on a fragrant blossom. It is a state of heightened awareness where we can observe the intricacies of our inner landscapes – the rustling of our thoughts, the surge of our emotions, and the delicate dance of sensations within our bodies – without becoming entangled in their narratives or overwhelmed by their intensity. Picture your mind as a vast, open sky, and mindfulness as the wondrous collage of clouds that drift across it, ever-changing yet fleeting, inviting us to step outside the confines of time and immerse ourselves in the eternal beauty of the now.

The Role of Mindfulness in Anxiety and Depression:

Both anxiety and depression often take root in the subconscious of our minds, sprouting from the seeds of past regrets or growing in future uncertainties. They thrive when we allow our thoughts to become entangled in a cycle of rumination when we incessantly replay past moments or fret about future outcomes. But fear not, for mindfulness is a transformative power, a beacon of light that gently guides our attention back to the present moment, like a lighthouse piercing through the dense fog. By shifting our focus away from the murky depths of the past or the distant horizons of the future, we break free from the suffocating grip of anxious thoughts and discover inner peace in the stillness and beauty of the present.

Benefits of Mindfulness for Anxiety and Depression:

The integration of mindfulness into our stress-management practice blesses us with a multitude of beneficial gifts, allowing us to reclaim our peace of mind and stride forward with confidence and grace:

1. **Increased self-awareness:** Through the practice of mindfulness, we embark on a profound journey of self-exploration, peering into the depths of our being. We learn to recognize and label anxiety-inducing thoughts and emotions, gaining a deeper understanding of our triggers and patterns. Like skilled explorers charting uncharted territories, we venture into the layers of our subconscious minds, illuminating our hidden corners and reclaiming our power.

2. **Reduced worry:** In the realm of mindfulness, we become the astute observer, donning the cloak of detachment and resilience. We no longer allow ourselves to be ensnared in the repetitive and unhelpful cycles of worry. Instead, we observe our thoughts with compassionate curiosity, watching them arise and dissipate like ripples on a serene pond. We gain the power to choose which thoughts to entertain and which to release, freeing ourselves from the clutches of depression's relentless grip.

3. **Enhanced emotional regulation:** Mindfulness empowers us to navigate the vast ocean of our emotions, guiding us through stormy seas with unwavering grace. We learn to acknowledge and accept our feelings,

no longer drowning in their overwhelming depths. With a gentle touch of self-compassion and wisdom, we respond to our emotions in a way that nourishes and uplifts our spirits, like a soothing balm for the weary soul.

4. Improved cognitive flexibility: As we delve deeper into the realms of mindfulness, our perspective broadens, expanding with acceptance and understanding. We see situations from different angles, contemplating their every vantage point. We open ourselves to alternative interpretations of our experiences, shedding the shackles of rigid thinking and welcoming the liberating dance of possibility and potential.

5. Increased resilience: The practice of mindfulness bestows upon us the invaluable gift of resilience, a superpower that propels us forward in the face of life's most significant challenges. With every breath and every moment of presence, we forge a shield of equanimity and adaptability. The storms of anxiety may rage, but we stand firm, rooted in the depths of our being, unwavering in our commitment to peace and harmony. Now, let us embark on a grand adventure through the realms of mindfulness, where we shall encounter a treasure trove of transformative exercises, each designed to deepen your awareness and diminish anxiety's grip on your life.

Mindfulness invites us to embark on a magnificent voyage of self-discovery and inner peace, a path strewn with blossoms of tranquility and serenity. It is not a magic potion that banishes anxiety entirely, but rather a profound practice that enables us to develop a healthier and more peaceful relationship with it. As you embrace the transformative journey outlined in this chapter, let the flames of curiosity and courage guide you into the dazzling realm of mindfulness. Allow yourself to be enchanted by its spell, for within its embrace lies the key to unlocking a world of deep calm and boundless compassion. Prepare yourself, brave traveler, and be **awed by the transformative power of mindfulness as an integral part of your life**. The adventure awaits, eager to unveil its treasures and gifts. With an open heart and a willing spirit, step onto this magical path of self-discovery and watch as your anxiety dissolves and depression vanishes, revealing the radiant essence of your most authentic self.

Body-Scan for Mindfulness

As you close your eyes and settle into a comfortable position, you begin the exercise by bringing your attention to the top of your head. Imagine a warm, soft light illuminating this area, inviting you to explore and scan your body with a sense of gentle curiosity.

As you travel down, notice any sensations you encounter along the way. Pay attention to your forehead, your eyebrows, and the space between your eyes. Release any tension you may find, allowing it to melt away with each exhale. Feel the relaxation spreading across your face like a gentle caress.

Continue descending, visiting your cheeks, your jaw, and your neck. Let go of any tightness or stiffness you may discover, welcoming a sensation of ease and comfort as you exhale. Feel the weight of your head gently sinking into the supportive cushion of your neck.

Moving further down, explore your shoulders, noticing any tension, knots, or areas of discomfort. With each breath, imagine you are breathing warmth and relaxation into these areas, allowing them to soften and release. Feel a sense of lightness and freedom as the tension dissolves, creating space for peace and tranquility.

Continue this mindful scan, traveling down to your arms, elbows, and hands. Let go of any tension or tightness you may encounter, surrendering and releasing with each breath. Feel a sense of warmth and relaxation flowing through your limbs, revitalizing and restoring balance.

As you journey further down, explore your chest and your abdomen. Notice the rise and fall of your breath, observing the sensation of each inhale and exhale. Allow your breath to nourish and ground you, bringing a sense of calm and centeredness to your entire being.

Travel down with your mind's eye and, notice your thighs, and release any build-up of tension with a deep exhalation, letting go of the moment. Notice your legs, knees, and ankles. Releasing and letting go of all lingering tension, feeling the gentle warmth of mindful awareness.

Finally, arrive at the tips of your toes, feeling the grounded connection they provide. Notice any sensations in your feet, letting go of any tension or discomfort you may come across. As you breathe, feel a sense of stability and rootedness, anchoring you in the present moment.

Take a moment to appreciate the journey you have taken through your body and the attention and care you have bestowed upon yourself. Feel a deep sense of relaxation, as if you are floating on a cloud of serenity, supported by the profound stillness within.

When you're ready, gently open your eyes, knowing that you can return to this mindful scan whenever you need to reconnect with your body and cultivate a sense of peace and presence. Carry this heightened awareness with you as you continue throughout your day, savoring the richness of each moment.

The Calm Mountain Lake

CLOSE YOUR EYES AND take a deep breath. Imagine yourself standing on a serene mountaintop, surrounded by lush greenery and a gentle breeze kissing your skin. As you open your eyes, you are captivated by the sight that lies before you - a crystal-clear lake nestled peacefully in the valley below.

Allow yourself to immerse yourself in the scene. Feel the solid ground beneath your feet, connecting you to the stability and strength of the mountain. As you continue to breathe deeply, you become aware of the coolness of the air, refreshing and invigorating your senses.

Observe the surface of the lake, still and undisturbed, reflecting the vibrant blue sky above. Its tranquility is infectious, soothing your racing mind. Every inch of your surroundings radiates calmness, and you cannot help but feel the weight of your anxiety begin to ease.

Take a slow, mindful step forward and start descending the mountain trail that winds its way down to the lake. As you walk, imagine that your worries and fears are melting away with every step you take, dissipating into the atmosphere. Picture them turning into colorful, fragile bubbles that gently float away, carried by the breeze.

As you reach the shore of the lake, you notice a small stone bench beckoning you to sit. Take a seat and allow yourself to surrender to the serenity of the moment. Notice the rhythmic sound of the water lapping against the rocks. Feel the warmth of the sunlight on your skin as it filters through the branches of the surrounding trees.

Now, let your awareness turn inward. Bring attention to your breath, the ebb and flow of each inhale and exhale. Feel the rise and fall of your chest, grounding you in the present moment. As your breathing deepens, you feel a sense of expansiveness, as if your breath is merging with the gentle movement of the lake itself.

Focus on the patterns forming on the surface of the water. Notice how they come and go, ever-changing and transient, just like your thoughts and anxieties. Allow them to drift away, to dissolve into the vastness of the lake.

Take a moment to appreciate the stillness that surrounds you. Allow your body and mind to relax, releasing any tension or tightness that may have held you captive.

As you sit there fully present in the moment, a sense of calm washes over you, like a slow, gentle wave gently cascading onto the shore. With each passing second, you feel more at ease, more connected to the eternal tranquility that resides within you.

Take as much time as you need in this visualization, allowing your mind to fully embrace the calmness of the mountain lake. When you are ready, gently bring your awareness back to the present moment, feeling refreshed and rejuvenated.

Remember, you can revisit this visualization whenever you need to find solace and peace. The calm mountain lake will always be there, patiently awaiting your return, ready to embrace you in its serene embrace.

CHAPTER FIVE

CBT
COGNITIVE-BEHAVIORAL
THERAPY

STRATEGIES FOR MANAGING AND UNDERSTANDING ANXIETY AND DEPRESSION

Surrender to what is. Let go of what was. Have faith in what will be. -Sonia Ricotti

I N THIS CHAPTER, WE will explore cognitive-behavioral strategies, which are highly effective in addressing anxious thoughts and behaviors. Cognitive-behavioral therapy (CBT) is a widely used and evidence-based approach that helps individuals recognize and challenge negative thought patterns and replace them with more balanced and realistic thinking. By applying these techniques, individuals can gain control over their anxiety and improve their overall well-being. This chapter will provide an overview of information on the principles of CBT and offer specific exercises to help you reduce stress and depression to regain a sense of control.

The basic principles of Cognitive-Behavioral Therapy (CBT):

Revolve around the understanding that our thoughts, emotions, and behaviors are interconnected. The cognitive model of anxiety explains that our thoughts or interpretations of situations contribute to the development and maintenance of anxiety and depression.

In CBT, it is believed that our thoughts play a significant role in shaping our emotions and behaviors. For example, if we hold negative or irrational thoughts about a situation, it can lead to heightened anxiety and negative emotions. On the other hand, if we have more positive and rational thoughts, it can lead to reduced stress and more adaptive behaviors.

In addition to addressing anxiety, cognitive-behavioral therapy (CBT) is also effective in managing symptoms of depression. The principles of CBT can be applied to identify and challenge negative thought patterns and behaviors that contribute to depressive symptoms.

Negative thinking patterns, such as self-criticism, bleak outlook, and belief in personal failure, are common in individuals experiencing depression. These thoughts can further perpetuate feelings of hopelessness, sadness, and low self-esteem. CBT works to replace these negative thoughts with more realistic and balanced thinking, leading to a reduction in depressive symptoms.

CBT for depression focuses on various techniques and strategies, including:

1. Cognitive Restructuring: This technique involves identifying and challenging negative and irrational thoughts that contribute to depression. Individuals can develop more rational and constructive beliefs by examining the evidence for and against these thoughts. For example, questioning the belief that "nothing ever goes right for me" and replacing it with "there have been times when things have gone well for me" can lead to a more positive outlook.

2. Behavioral Activation: Depression often leads to a decrease in pleasurable activities and social interactions. **Behavioral activation** involves identifying and engaging in activities that bring joy, accomplishment, and a sense of fulfillment. By increasing participation in positive activities, individuals can counteract the negative impact of depression on their mood and motivation.

3. Graded Exposure: This technique involves gradually facing situations or activities that are avoided due to depression. By exposing themselves to these situations in a controlled and supportive manner, individuals can reduce avoidance and build confidence in their ability to cope.

4. Problem-Solving Skills: Depression can impair problem-solving abilities, leading to a sense of helplessness and exacerbating symptoms. CBT helps individuals develop effective problem-solving skills by breaking down problems into manageable steps, generating alternative solutions, and evaluating their effectiveness.

5. Relaxation Techniques: Stress and anxiety often accompany depression. Learning and practicing relaxation techniques, such as progressive muscle relaxation, deep breathing, and guided imagery, can help individuals manage stress and promote a sense of calm.

6. Thought Monitoring: This technique involves keeping a record of negative thoughts and the situations that trigger them. By becoming aware of these patterns, individuals can gain insight into the triggers and underlying beliefs that contribute to their depressive symptoms.

7. Cognitive Distortions: CBT addresses common cognitive distortions or thinking errors that contribute to depression, such as all-or-nothing thinking, overgeneralization, and mind reading. By recognizing these distortions, individuals can challenge them and develop more balanced and realistic thinking patterns.

8. Gradual Goal Setting: Setting small, achievable goals is an essential aspect of CBT for depression. By deliberately working towards specific goals, individuals can experience a sense of accomplishment, boost their self-confidence, and improve their overall mood.

9. Social Skills Training: Depression can often lead to social withdrawal and difficulties in interpersonal relationships. CBT may include training in effective communication, assertiveness, and problem-solving skills to improve social interactions and relationships.

10. Homework Assignments: CBT sessions often include homework assignments to reinforce and practice the skills learned in therapy. These assignments may involve practicing relaxation techniques, engaging in pleasurable activities, or challenging negative thoughts.

11. Relapse Prevention: CBT emphasizes developing strategies to prevent relapse and maintain progress over the long term. This may include identifying early warning signs, creating a relapse prevention plan, and incorporating ongoing self-care and coping strategies.

It's important to note that CBT is a collaborative and active therapy approach. The therapist works collaboratively with the individual, providing guidance, support, and feedback throughout the process. CBT is typically conducted over a structured number of sessions, although the duration can vary depending on individual needs.

By incorporating these CBT techniques into our daily lives, individuals with anxiety and depression can work toward challenging negative thought patterns and develop more adaptive coping strategies. However, it is important to note that CBT is most effective when guided by a trained mental health professional. They can provide individualized guidance and support throughout the therapy process.

Cognitive distortions:

These are common thinking patterns that are often automatic and subconscious. These patterns of thinking can contribute to anxiety and other negative emotions. **By recognizing and challenging these distortions, individuals can develop a more accurate and balanced perspective, reducing their distress.**

1. Catastrophizing: This cognitive distortion involves magnifying the negative aspects of a situation and imagining the worst possible outcome. For example, if someone receives criticism at work, they may catastrophize by thinking they will be fired and end up homeless. This distortion can intensify anxiety and make it difficult to cope with everyday challenges.

2. Overgeneralization: Overgeneralization involves making sweeping negative conclusions based on a single event. For example, if someone fails a test, they may overgeneralize by thinking they're a complete failure in all aspects of life. This distortion overlooks other positive experiences and reinforces negative self-perceptions.

3. Personalization: This distortion involves assuming excessive personal responsibility or blame for events that are beyond one's control. For example, if a friend cancels plans, someone who engages in personalization may immediately think it's their fault, and their friend doesn't want to spend time with them. This distortion can lead to low self-esteem and unnecessary self-blame.

Other common cognitive distortions include:

4. All-or-nothing Thinking: This distortion involves seeing things in black and white without recognizing shades of gray. For example, someone may believe they're a complete failure if they're not perfect. This can lead to feelings of disappointment, inadequacy, and anxiety.

5. Mental Filtering: This distortion involves selectively focusing only on negative aspects of a situation while ignoring positive aspects. For example, someone may discount compliments they receive and only concentrate on the criticism they receive, reinforcing negative self-perceptions.

In cognitive-behavioral therapy (CBT), therapists help individuals identify and challenge these cognitive distortions. By examining the evidence and evaluating the accuracy and intensity of their thoughts, individuals can develop more balanced and realistic thinking patterns. This process often involves questioning the evidence for their distorted thoughts, considering alternative explanations, and creating more adaptive and healthier thought patterns. The ultimate goal is to empower individuals to gain control over their thoughts and emotions and improve their overall well-being.

The ABC model: Cracking the Code to Anxiety and Depression:

Unlocking the secrets to understanding the relationship between activating events, beliefs, and consequences.

Utilizing Thought Diaries:

You assess and track your thoughts through diaries or tools that help you gain insight into your unwanted thought patterns.

1. Assessing and Tracking Thoughts:

2. Uncovering the Patterns of Your Mind:

Keeping a thought diary is like a window into depression and anxiety. Discover how writing down your thoughts in specific situations can help you gain insight into your anxiety by identifying triggers and patterns. This allows you to **"Crack the Anxiety Code"** by uncovering the recurring thoughts and emotions associated with stressors in your life.

Awareness leads to understanding, leading to that "Ah Ha" moment and allowing you to finally take charge of your anxiety and depression.

By using thought diaries and tracking tools to become more aware of your thoughts and emotions, you can see the root causes of your anxiety and why it was there in the first place. You can begin to understand and have compassion for those thoughts that only wanted to protect you. Now, through a clear awareness of how anxiety and depression manifest. You can now decide if it's appropriate for this moment. If not, keep observing and fearlessly recording non-judgmentally and watch as anxiety's power over you diminishes.

Cognitive-behavioral therapy (CBT) provides practical tools for managing anxiety and depression.

Your thoughts play a crucial role in shaping your emotions and behaviors.

Cognitive distortions are irrational thoughts that contribute to anxiety and can cause depression.

Now, with that basic understanding of the ABC model in **Cognitive-Behavioral Therapy,** let's dive a little deeper and see with examples how this might benefit understanding the causes and outcomes of symptoms.

The ABC model helps you understand the relationship between your **Activating events (A), your Beliefs and interpretations (B), and your emotional and behavioral Consequences (C).**

1. Activating Events (A): What Sets Off Your Anxiety?

Identify the triggers or situations that ignite your anxiety. These are the events or circumstances that cause you to feel anxious. Examples include public speaking, meeting new people, or a work deadline.

2. Beliefs and Interpretations (B): The Power of Your Thoughts:

Unravel the thoughts and perceptions associated with your activating events. These are your beliefs or interpretations about the situation that trigger your anxiety. They can be rational or irrational. Examples of irrational beliefs include "If I make a mistake during my presentation, everyone will think I'm incompetent" or "If I don't do well in this interview, I'm a failure."

3. Emotional and Behavioral Consequences (C): Analyzing Your Reactions:

Explore how your thoughts and beliefs shape your emotional and behavioral responses. Your beliefs influence your reactions to activating events, which can range from anxiety to panic attacks to avoidance behaviors. For example, suppose you believe that making a mistake in a presentation will lead to embarrassment and a negative evaluation from others. In that case, you might experience intense anxiety, have difficulty concentrating, or even choose to avoid public speaking altogether.

To use the ABC method practically, follow these steps:

1. Identify the activating event (A): Recognize the trigger or situation that causes your anxiety. Please write it down or mentally note it.

2. Identify your beliefs and interpretations (B): Take a moment to reflect on the thoughts and perceptions that arise when you think about the activating event. Ask yourself, "What do I believe about this situation? What thoughts are running through my mind?" Write down these thoughts and beliefs, being as specific as possible.

3. Analyze your emotional and behavioral consequences (C): Notice how your thoughts and beliefs about the activating event influence your emotions and behaviors. For example, ask yourself, "How does this belief make me feel? How am I reacting or behaving because of it?" Write down any emotional or behavioral consequences you experience.

4. Challenge irrational beliefs: Examine your beliefs and thoughts to determine if they are rational or realistic. Ask yourself, "Is there evidence supporting this belief? Are there alternative explanations or interpretations?" Look for evidence contradicting your irrational beliefs and challenge them with more balanced and realistic thoughts. Get outside help. It doesn't hurt to get a second pair of trusted eyes on anything uncomfortable.

5. Replace with rational beliefs: Once you've identified and challenged your irrational beliefs, replace them with more sensible and helpful thoughts. For example, if your belief is "If I don't do well in this interview, I'm a failure," a more rational belief could be, "Even if I don't get this job, it doesn't define my worth or abilities. There will be other opportunities."

By practicing the ABC method regularly, you can gain a better understanding of how your thoughts contribute to your feelings of stress. **Challenging and replacing irrational beliefs** with more rational ones can help you reduce anxious thoughts and develop more adaptive emotional and behavioral responses.

Assessing and tracking thoughts involves recording your thoughts and emotions in specific situations that trigger anxiety or depression. This can be done using a thought diary or a tracking tool, such as a journal or an app on your phone.

Here's how to use this method for both:

1. Start by recognizing and noting down situations that make you feel anxious: These could be situations like speaking in public, going to a social gathering, or facing a challenging task at work.

Example: Going to a party where you don't know many people.

2. Pay attention to your thoughts and write them down in the diary or tracking tool. Be as specific as possible. Write down any negative or worrisome thoughts that come to mind.

Example: "Nobody will talk to me," "They'll think I'm boring," "What if I say something stupid?"

3. Keep track of any patterns or recurring thoughts you notice: Are specific themes or beliefs that tend to come up repeatedly? Identifying these patterns can help you understand the underlying causes of your anxiety.

Example: You notice that you often have thoughts about being judged or rejected by others.

4. Monitor the intensity of your emotions in different situations: Rate your anxiety on a scale of 1-10, with ten being the most intense. This helps you gauge the impact of your thoughts on your emotions.

Example: Before going to the party, you rate your anxiety as an 8.

5. Regularly review your thought diary or tracking tool to gain insights into your anxiety triggers. Look for any patterns or common themes that emerge. This awareness will allow you to understand better the underlying factors contributing to your anxiety.

Example: You notice that your anxiety is consistently triggered by social situations where you fear being judged or rejected.

6. Use this awareness to take appropriate steps to manage your anxiety effectively: Once you understand your **triggers** and **thought patterns,** you can develop coping strategies. These could include challenging negative thoughts, practicing relaxation techniques, seeking support from others, or gradually facing your fears through exposure therapy.

Example: **You challenge your negative thoughts by reminding yourself that not everyone will judge you and that it's okay to make mistakes in social situations. You also practice deep breathing exercises and remind yourself of past successful social interactions.**

By consistently assessing and tracking your thoughts and emotions, you can become more aware of the factors contributing to your perception. This increased awareness empowers you to make positive changes and develop effective strategies for managing distressful situations.

The key points to remember in this brief outline are the benefits of using **Cognitive-Behavioral Therapy** in helping with stress management:

- COGNITIVE-BEHAVIORAL THERAPY (CBT) PROVIDES PRACTICAL TOOLS FOR MANAGING ANXIETY AND DEPRESSION.

- YOUR THOUGHTS PLAY A CRUCIAL ROLE IN SHAPING YOUR EMOTIONS AND BEHAVIORS.

- COGNITIVE DISTORTIONS ARE IRRATIONAL THOUGHTS THAT CONTRIBUTE TO ANXIETY AND DEPRESSION.

- THE ABC MODEL HELPS YOU UNDERSTAND THE RELATIONSHIP BETWEEN ACTIVATING EVENTS, BELIEFS, AND CONSEQUENCES.

- ASSESSING AND TRACKING YOUR THOUGHTS THROUGH DIARIES OR TOOLS HELPS YOU GAIN INSIGHT INTO YOUR STRESSOR PATTERNS.

All of the tools that effectively treat anxiety or depression point to one common denominator, *"stressor awareness"* with **non-judgmental awareness.** Know your anxiety and depression; don't let anxious thoughts run on autopilot. **Take control and make a safe landing!**

THE MAGIC GOLDEN KEY

ONCE UPON A TIME, in a bustling city surrounded by towering skyscrapers and bustling streets, there was a young woman named Emily. Emily was a constant worrier, plagued by anxiety that held her back from thoroughly enjoying her life. Every day, she felt a heavy weight on her shoulders, as if she were trapped in a never-ending cycle of fear and doubt.

One evening, as Emily sat in her cozy apartment, bathed in the warm glow of candlelight, she stumbled upon an ancient book hidden among the dusty shelves of her bookcase. Curiosity overtaking her, she blew off the thick layer of dust and opened it to reveal a golden key tucked within its pages, with intricate symbols etched onto its surface.

Intrigued, Emily took the key and examined it closely. She could feel a mysterious energy emanating from it, as if it held the power to unlock something within herself. Determined to find out its purpose, she set off on a quest to discover the secret behind the key.

As she walked through the darkened city streets, Emily noticed a faint glow in the corner of her eye. Following the glow, she found herself in front of an ancient, ornately carved door between two towering buildings. Without hesitation, she inserted the golden key into the lock, and with a gentle turn, the door creaked open.

Stepping inside, Emily found herself in a lush, vibrant garden filled with blooming flowers of every color imaginable. The air was filled with the sweet scent of lavender and the soft whispers of the wind. As she wandered further into the garden, she discovered a magical fountain at the heart of it all.

The fountain's water sparkled and shimmered, reflecting the moonlight and stars above. Drawn to its ethereal beauty, Emily approached the fountain and saw her reflection staring back at her. But this reflection was different. It was filled with confidence and a sense of calm.

As Emily peered into the water, she saw her worries and anxieties swirling within it. She realized that she had the power to control these emotions, just as she had the power to control the key that had led her here. With a deep breath, she extended her hand and touched the water, instantly feeling a surge of tranquility wash over her.

The moment Emily made contact with the water, the garden around her began to transform. Vines grew rapidly, weaving themselves into a grand green staircase that stretched out before her. Intrigued and determined, Emily stepped into the enveloping vines, navigating their twists and turns confidently and determinedly.

With each step she took, the vines responded, guiding her through the maze. As she progressed, she encountered various challenges and obstacles, symbolic of the fears and worries that had held her captive for so long. But instead of succumbing to them, Emily faced them head-on, using her newfound courage and resilience to overcome them.

With each obstacle conquered, the vines seemed to grow stronger, creating a path of empowerment for Emily. She realized that the more control she exerted over her worries, the more control she gained over her own life. As she reached the center of the labyrinth, she stood amidst a breathtaking panorama of mountaintops bathed in the golden light of the rising sun.

At that moment, Emily understood that she held the key to her own happiness and well-being. She had the power to choose how her story would unfold, and her anxiety would no longer define her. With a sense of liberation and gratitude, she made a promise to herself to face each day with courage, embracing the unknown with an open heart.

Leaving the garden with a newfound sense of purpose, Emily realized that her journey was not over. Armed with the wisdom gained from her experience, she made it her mission to help others who were trapped in the cycle of anxiety, showing them that they, too, held the key to their own liberation.

And so Emily ventured back into the city, spreading hope and inspiration wherever she went. Through her stories and acts of kindness, she taught others the power of visualization, the magic of imagination, and the strength that could be gained by taking control of one's fears.

In the end, Emily's personal journey became a guiding light of inspiration for those struggling with anxiety, reminding them that a brighter, more peaceful path was always within reach if they were willing to take the first step. And with each flicker of the golden key, the world became slightly brighter, one person at a time.

Dear Reader,

I hope you are enjoying this book as much as I have enjoyed writing it. There are many chapters ahead, and I think you will find all of them beneficial in some way. Right now, at this point in the book, I would really appreciate it if you would take a moment to write a review for this book. It would help others discover some of our shared magic so far! I want to know what you like most. **Simply SCAN** with your camera directly to the **Amazon Review page.**

Scan me

https://amzn.to/43YX0cU

Where you can quickly leave a review: https://amzn.to/43YX0cU
Thank you for taking this healing journey with me.

My heart hopes and prays for our serenity and happiness in each and every moment. -Lillyin Love (CHECK-IN)

CHAPTER SIX

FOOD/DIET NOURISHING YOUR MIND-BODY AND SPIRIT

HOW FOOD AND DIET AFFECT ANXIETY AND DEPRESSION

When I let go of what I am, I become what I might be. -Lao Tzu

IN THIS CHAPTER, WE will explore the fascinating connection between food and stress management. A growing body of research has shown that diet plays a significant role in mental health, including anxiety levels. The food we consume can either promote or decrease depression symptoms by affecting neurotransmitter production, hormonal balance, inflammation levels, and gut health. By making **mindful choices** about our diet and incorporating stress-reducing foods, we can positively impact our mental and emotional well-being.

The Gut-Brain Connection:

The gut-brain connection refers to the bidirectional communication between our gastrointestinal system and our brain. The state of our gut microbiome, the complex ecosystem of bacteria that reside in our intestines, has a profound influence on our mental health. Imbalances in the gut microbiome can contribute to inflammation, hormonal dysregulation, and neurotransmitter imbalances, all of which can increase the risk of anxiety and other mental health disorders.

Anxiety-Inducing Foods:

Certain foods and drinks can exacerbate anxiety symptoms and cause depression. They should be consumed in **moderation**, including:

1. Caffeine: A stimulant can increase feelings of jitteriness and restlessness and cause sleep disturbances. Individuals with anxiety are often more sensitive to the effects of caffeine and may benefit from reducing their intake.

2. Sugar: High sugar intake can lead to blood sugar fluctuations, energy crashes, and inflammation, which can contribute to anxiety symptoms and mood swings. Refined sugars found in processed foods should be limited, while natural sugars from fruits can be a healthier alternative.

3. Alcohol: While alcohol may temporarily reduce anxiety symptoms, it is a depressant that can disrupt sleep, decrease overall mood, and lead to increased depressive cycles over time.

4. Processed Foods: Highly processed foods, such as fast food, chips, and sugary snacks, are often high in unhealthy fats, sugars, and artificial additives. These ingredients can negatively impact brain health and contribute to inflammation, which can worsen anxiety symptoms. Opt for whole, unprocessed foods that nourish your body and provide essential nutrients.

5. High-Fat Foods: While healthy fats, such as those found in avocados, nuts, and seeds, are beneficial for brain health, consuming excessive amounts of saturated and trans fats can lead to inflammation and increase the risk of anxiety and mood disorders. Limit your intake of foods like fried and fatty meats, processed foods, and full-fat dairy products.

6. Artificial Sweeteners: Artificial sweeteners found in diet sodas, sugar-free snacks, and low-calorie products can negatively impact gut health, which has been linked to anxiety and mood disorders. They may also disrupt natural hunger cues and lead to overeating. In moderation, opt for natural sweeteners like stevia, honey, or maple syrup.

7. High Sodium Foods: Consuming excessive amounts of sodium, often found in processed foods, can lead to increased blood pressure and contribute to feelings of anxiety. High sodium intake can also lead to bloating and water retention, which may increase feelings of discomfort and stress. Choose low-sodium options and flavor your food with herbs and spices instead.

Remember that making dietary changes alone may not completely alleviate anxiety symptoms. However, adopting a balanced and nourishing diet can support overall well-being and complement other strategies for anxiety management. Consult a healthcare professional or registered dietitian for personalized dietary recommendations and guidance.

Anxiety-Reducing Foods:

Conversely, incorporating certain foods into your diet can help reduce anxiety symptoms and promote mental well-being, including:

1. Omega-3 fatty acids: Found in fatty fish such as salmon, mackerel, and sardines, as well as walnuts and flaxseeds, omega-3 fatty acids have been shown to reduce inflammation and support brain health. They may also help regulate neurotransmitters involved in mood regulation, such as serotonin.

2. Complex carbohydrates: Foods like whole grains, legumes, and starchy vegetables provide a steady release of glucose into the bloodstream, promoting stable energy levels and mood. They also contain essential nutrients and fiber that support overall brain health.

3. Green leafy vegetables: Nutrient-rich vegetables such as spinach, kale, and broccoli are packed with vitamins, minerals, and antioxidants. These reduce inflammation and support brain health, positively impacting stress symptoms.

4. Fermented foods: Foods like yogurt, sauerkraut, and kimchi are rich in probiotics, which promote a healthy gut microbiome. A balanced gut microbiome has been linked to improved mental health and reduced anxiety symptoms.

5. Herbal teas: Certain herbal teas, such as chamomile, lavender, and lemon balm, have calming properties that can help reduce anxiety and promote relaxation. Close your eyes and envision a serene garden bathed in golden sunlight, where the delicate fragrance of **chamomile, lavender, lemon balm, and bergamot herbs** wafts through the air. Each of these herbal teas carries with it a unique set of therapeutic benefits, offering a respite from the storm of anxiety and depression.

Mindful Eating Habits:

In addition to incorporating anxiety-reducing foods, adopting mindful eating habits can further support mental well-being:

1. Eat regular meals: Maintaining a regular eating schedule can help stabilize blood sugar levels, energy, and mood throughout the day. However, there is a growing body of research that supports "intermittant-fasting" for healthy individuals as way to boost your immune system.

2. Avoid skipping meals: Skipping meals can lead to drops in blood sugar levels, causing irritability, fatigue, and increased anxiety and depression.

3. Practice portion control: Pay attention to portion sizes and eat mindfully, focusing on the taste, texture, and satisfaction derived from eating slowly. Taking time to savor and enjoy each bite, chewing it thoroughly, which in turn only adds to your enjoyment and countless other health benefits.

4. Stay hydrated: Dehydration can contribute to symptoms of anxiety. Ensure you are drinking enough water throughout the day to support optimal brain function reducing anxiety and depression. Most people forget just how important getting plenty of water can be, affecting all aspects of life, remember water is life.

Affirmations to Nourish Mind-Body and Spirit

1. I NOURISH MY BODY WITH HEALTHY, WHOLE FOODS, FUELING IT WITH THE NUTRIENTS IT NEEDS TO THRIVE.

2. I MAKE MINDFUL CHOICES WHEN IT COMES TO WHAT I EAT, HONORING MY BODY'S UNIQUE NEEDS AND PREFERENCES.

3. I LISTEN TO MY BODY'S HUNGER AND FULLNESS CUES, EATING WHEN I AM HUNGRY AND STOPPING WHEN I AM SATISFIED.

4. I ENJOY A BALANCED AND VARIED DIET, APPRECIATING THE ABUNDANCE OF DELICIOUS AND NUTRITIOUS FOODS AVAILABLE TO ME.

5. I RELEASE ANY GUILT OR SHAME AROUND FOOD AND EMBRACE A POSITIVE AND LOVING RELATIONSHIP WITH NOURISHMENT.

6. I CHOOSE FOODS THAT SUPPORT MY OVERALL WELL-BEING AND PROMOTE OPTIMAL HEALTH AND VITALITY.

7. I FIND JOY IN PREPARING AND COOKING MY OWN MEALS, IN-FUSING THEM WITH LOVE AND INTENTION.

8. I AM GRATEFUL FOR THE NOURISHMENT THAT FOOD PROVIDES, UNDERSTANDING THE PRIVILEGE IT IS TO HAVE ACCESS TO SUSTE-NANCE.

9. I PRIORITIZE SELF-CARE BY TAKING THE TIME TO SIT DOWN AND SAVOR MY MEALS, ALLOWING MYSELF TO ENJOY AND APPRECIATE THEM FULLY.

10. I TRUST MY BODY'S WISDOM IN KNOWING WHAT IT NEEDS AND HONOR ITS SIGNALS AND CRAVINGS WITH COMPASSION AND UNDERSTANDING.

AROMATHERAPY

AROMATHERAPY AND THE USE of certain herbs have been found to be effective in helping to alleviate anxiety symptoms and lighten depression. These natural remedies work by stimulating the olfactory system or through the active compounds found in the herbs. Here is a breakdown of how aromatherapy and herbs can help with anxiety and depression:

1. Aromatherapy oils:

Aromatherapy utilizes essential oils extracted from plants to promote emotional and physical well-being. When inhaled or applied topically, these oils can directly affect the limbic system, which is responsible for emotions and memory. Aromatherapy can help with anxiety in the following ways:

a. Calming Effects: Certain essential oils, such as lavender, chamomile, and bergamot, have calming and soothing properties. Inhaling these oils or using them in a diffuser can help reduce anxiety and promote a sense of relaxation and tranquility.

b. Stress Relief: Essential oils like **ylang-ylang, clary sage, and frankincense** have been shown to help reduce stress levels and promote a more balanced emotional state. Using these oils in a diffuser, massage oil, or bath can help alleviate negative emotions.

c. Improved Sleep: Anxiety can often disrupt sleep patterns, exacerbating symptoms. Essential oils like **lavender, vetiver, and sandalwood** are known for their sedative properties and can help promote better sleep quality when used in a diffuser or applied topically before bed.

2. Herbs:

Certain herbs contain compounds that have natural anxiolytic (anxiety-reducing) effects. These compounds work by interacting with neurotransmitters in the brain, promoting relaxation and reducing anxiety symptoms. Here are some commonly used herbs for anxiety: **Ashwagandha, Chamomile, Valerian Root, Passionflower, and Lemon Balm:**

Ashwagandha:

This adaptogenic herb helps the body adapt to stress and has been shown to reduce anxiety levels. It can be taken in capsule form or consumed as a tea.

Chamomile:

Chamomile is a gentle herb with calming properties. It can be consumed as a tea or taken in supplement form to reduce anxiety and promote relaxation.

Valerian Root:

Valerian root has mild sedative properties and can help reduce anxiety and promote better sleep. It is commonly consumed as a tea or in capsule form.

Passionflower:

Passionflower is an herb traditionally used for its calming and anxiety-reducing effects. It can be consumed as a tea or taken as a supplement.

Lemon Balm:

Lemon balm has a calming effect on the nervous system and can help reduce stress and promote relaxation. It can be consumed as a tea or taken in capsule form.

In addition to herbs for anxiety, there are also herbs that can be beneficial for depression. These **herbs** are often used to support emotional well-being and help alleviate symptoms of depression. Here are some commonly used herbs for depression: **St. Johns wort, Saffron, Rhodiola Rosea, Lavender, and Ginseng:**

St. John's Wort:

St. John's Wort is a well-known herb for depression. It has been extensively studied and has shown effectiveness in reducing mild to moderate depressive symptoms. It can be taken in capsule form or consumed as a tea.

Saffron:

Saffron is a spice derived from the flower Crocus sativus. It has been used traditionally for its mood-enhancing properties and has shown promise in reducing symptoms of depression. It can be taken as a supplement.

Rhodiola Rosea:

Rhodiola Rosea is an adaptogenic herb that helps the body cope with stress and improve energy levels. It has been found to have mood-boosting effects and can be helpful for individuals with mild to moderate depression. It is commonly taken in capsule form.

Lavender:

Lavender is known for its calming and relaxing properties. It can help ease anxiety symptoms and promote a sense of well-being, which can be beneficial for individuals with depression. Lavender essential oil can be used in aromatherapy or diluted for topical application.

Ginseng:

Ginseng is an adaptogenic herb that has been used traditionally to improve mental and physical fatigue. It can help support mood and boost energy levels, making it helpful for individuals with depression. It can be taken in capsule form or consumed as a tea.

It's important to note that while these herbs can be supportive, they should not replace professional treatment for depression. If you or someone you know is experiencing symptoms of depression, it's essential to seek guidance from a healthcare professional for a comprehensive treatment plan.

Cannabidiol (CBD):

The pros and cons of using CBD for anxiety and depression:

The Pros:

1. Potential Anxiety Relief: Many individuals have reported experiencing a reduction in anxiety symptoms after incorporating CBD into their daily routine. CBD interacts with the endocannabinoid system in the body, which plays a role in regulating mood, stress, and anxiety levels. By promoting relaxation and calmness, CBD may help alleviate anxiety and offer some relief for depression.

2. Natural Approach: CBD is derived from the cannabis plant, but it does not contain the psychoactive compound THC, which is responsible for the "high" associated with marijuana. This means that CBD can provide potential benefits without inducing intoxicating effects. For individuals seeking a natural remedy for anxiety, CBD offers an alternative to traditional pharmaceuticals.

3. Few Side Effects: Compared to many pharmaceutical medications used to treat anxiety, CBD is generally well-tolerated and has minimal side effects. Some individuals may experience mild side effects such as dry mouth, drowsiness, or changes in appetite, but these are typically mild and temporary.

The Cons:

1. Lack of Regulation: The CBD industry is still largely unregulated, leading to product quality and potency inconsistency. This makes it crucial for consumers to do thorough research and purchase CBD products from reputable sources to ensure they are getting a safe and effective product.

2. Individual Variability: While CBD may be effective for many individuals, its efficacy can vary from person to person. Factors such as the severity of anxiety, dosage, and individual biochemistry can influence how well CBD works for each person. Finding the right dosage and product may require some trial and error.

3. Limited Research: Although there is growing evidence suggesting the potential benefits of CBD for anxiety, more research is needed to fully understand its effects and long-term implications. While many anecdotal reports are promising, larger-scale clinical trials are necessary to establish CBD's efficacy and safety more definitively. Ultimately, the decision to use CBD for anxiety should be made in consultation with a healthcare professional who can provide personalized guidance based on individual circumstances and medical history.

It's important to note that while **aromatherapy** and **herbs** can be helpful for managing anxiety, they should not replace professional medical advice or treatment. It's always a good idea to consult with a healthcare provider before incorporating these practices into your routine, especially if you have any pre-existing conditions or are taking medications.

Our food and diet play a significant role in our mental and emotional well-being. By understanding the impact of food on anxiety levels and incorporating anxiety-reducing foods into our diet, we can support our mental health and overall well-being. Additionally, **adopting mindful eating habits** can enhance our relationship with food and promote a balanced mood.

Vegetable and Herb Garden Oasis

CLOSE YOUR EYES AND imagine a peaceful oasis in your backyard, filled with the vibrant colors and intoxicating scents of a vegetable and herb garden. Picture yourself stepping onto the fertile earth, feeling the soft soil beneath your bare feet and the sun's warm rays kissing your skin. As you take a deep breath, the fragrant aroma of freshly turned earth and growing plants fills your senses, instantly transporting you to a place of tranquility and connection with nature.

Standing at the entrance of your garden, you gaze upon the canvas of possibilities before you. Rows of neatly prepared soil stretch out in front of you, ready to be adorned with an array of luscious vegetables and aromatic herbs. The anticipation fills your heart with joy as you envision the bountiful harvest that awaits.

With gentle hands, you tenderly sow the seeds into the earth, each a precious promise of life and nourishment. The soil eagerly receives them, its rich nutrients embracing the tiny seeds and nurturing their growth. You imagine the first delicate sprouts pushing through the soil's embrace, reaching toward the sun's warm caress.

From this moment on, you enter into a dance of partnership with nature and her magical forces.

As days become weeks, you watch with wonder and excitement as your garden transforms. Tender green shoots emerge, growing stronger with each passing day. The garden becomes your pallet of colors, with the vibrant hues of lettuce and spinach, the deep purples of eggplants and radicchio, and the fiery reds of ripe tomatoes and bell peppers. The fragrance of basil, rosemary, and mint fills the air, enticing you to come closer and savor their aromatic presence.

You become attuned to the needs of your plants, nurturing them like a doting parent. You eagerly tend to them, gently pulling out pesky weeds threatening their growth. Your fingers brush against the soft leaves, releasing their distinct fragrances and leaving a sense of calm in your wake. With every touch, you feel a deep connection to the earth and the life cycles that unfold within your garden.

As the weeks become months, your garden becomes a sanctuary, a place of solace and reflection. You spend mornings drinking home-made herbal teas amidst the plants, soaking in the beauty and serenity of their presence. You marvel at the intricate patterns of nature's design, the delicate veins of a cucumber leaf, and the complex symmetry of a sunflower's petals. Your garden becomes a testament to the resilience and beauty of life, reminding you of the miracles that can be nurtured from a single seed.

Finally, the time arrives to harvest the fruits of your labor. With a basket in hand, you stroll through the garden, gathering the ripe produce that nature has bestowed upon you. The vibrant colors and fragrant aromas become a celebration of abundance and gratitude.

At that moment, you realize that gardening is not just about cultivating plants; it is about growing your spirit, grounding yourself in the wonders of nature, and reconnecting with the simplicity and beauty of life.

So, as you open your eyes and return to the present moment, carry this vision of your vegetable and herb garden with you. Let it inspire you to create a personal oasis of beauty and nourishment. Know that by planting and tending to your garden, you are growing food and cultivating a sense of peace, connection, and harmony with the world around you.

Chapter Seven

Exercise Movement Towards Calm

Unleashing the Transformative Power of Exercise in Managing Anxiety and Depression

Exercise gives you endorphins. Endorphins make you happy. -Elle Woods (Legally Blonde)

AS WE CONTINUE OUR **journey** into the realm of managing stress, we come across an often-overlooked secret weapon – exercise. Most of us are familiar with the physical benefits of exercise, like shedding pounds, boosting cardiovascular health, and increasing strength. But have you ever pondered the incredible mental and emotional benefits it can bring? Numerous studies have shown that regular exercise can significantly reduce anxiety symptoms, elevate mood, and foster overall well-being. **We open the door to a tranquil and serene existence by weaving exercise into our daily lives.**

The Connection Between Exercise Helping Anxiety and Depression:

Prepare to be amazed as we explore how exercise works its magic on both mind and body, serving as a powerful remedy for anxiety and depression.

1. **NEUROCHEMICAL CHANGES**: Exercise has the remarkable ability to rouse your brain and body, stimulating the release of endorphins, dopamine, and serotonin. These neurotransmitters, renowned for their mood-enhancing prowess, work their wonders, significantly reducing anxiety and depression.

2. **STRESS REDUCTION**: Engaging in physical activity provides an escape hatch for stress and tension. As you immerse yourself in exercise, cortisol levels – the notorious stress hormones – dwindle, leaving behind a welcoming haven of relaxation.

3. **INCREASED SELF-CONFIDENCE**: Regular exercise ignites a spark of confidence within, sculpting a positive self-image. As you witness your physical abilities grow, self-esteem blossoms, radiating onto your outlook on life; with newfound assurance, anxiety retreats in defeat, and depression runs away.

4. **DISTRACTION FROM ANXIOUS THOUGHTS**: Meet anxiety's worst enemy – exercise. As you dive into your favorite form of physical activity, depression-ridden thoughts dissipate into oblivion. Your focus shifts to the present moment, embracing the exhilarating sensation of your muscles at work.

5. **BETTER SLEEP**: Anxiety often sabotages a restful night's slumber. But have no fear! Regular exercise has arrived as your knight in shining armor, ready to free you from the clutches of sleepless nights. By lulling your tired body into a state of deep rest, exercise banishes depression and gifts you with the rejuvenation you seek.

Beneficial Exercises for Unleashing Anxiety and Depression Relief:

Now, let us unveil a treasure chest of exercises carefully crafted to dismantle anxiety's stronghold and depression's dominion to usher in a landscape of golden tranquility.

1. Aerobic Exercise: Step into a world of elevated heart rates and oxygen-rich air. While galloping alongside brisk walks, lung-expanding jogs, graceful strokes in the water, or the rhythmic hum of cycling, your body releases endorphins, granting you a euphoric state of well-being.

2. Yoga: Prepare to embrace the mesmerizing dance of mind and body. Through yoga's artful blend of physical postures, breathwork, and meditation, your spirit ascends to a tranquil realm. Flexibility, strength, and balance join forces to create a sanctuary of serenity and peace.

3. Tai Chi: Unlock the ancient secrets of **tai chi** as you sway through gentle, flowing movements. With every deliberate step and deep breath, your body dips into relaxation mode, guiding you toward heightened body awareness and laser-sharp mental clarity. Anxiety dissipates, and depression fades, gradually replaced by an aura of calm.

4. Dancing: Let the rhythm guide your feet as you embark on a journey of self-expression through dance. In classes or freestyle, your body becomes a conduit for endorphin surges and tension release. Embrace the exuberance of dance, leaving anxiety and depression in the dust.

5. Mindful Walking: Step into nature's embrace as you embark on a mindful walking practice. Engross yourself in the present moment, savoring the sensations that arise within your body. As you walk amidst serene landscapes, worry unravels. It is replaced by a profound connection with nature's peaceful allure.

6. High-Intensity Interval Training (HIIT): Unleash your inner warrior as short bursts of intense exercise mingle with moments of recovery. HIIT workouts surge through your veins, thrusting you into exhilaration. In this energetic dance, your mood soars, cardiovascular health flourishes, and endorphins flood your system, diminishing depression's grip.

Incorporating Exercise into Daily Life:

Ah, the grand challenge – carving out time and motivation for exercise, particularly while wrestling with anxiety and depression. But fear not! With a few strategic moves, bringing exercise into your daily routine becomes a joyful act of self-care.

1. Start small and be consistent: Begin this venture with a gentle touch, dipping your toes into manageable exercise sessions. Gradually amplify the duration and intensity, luxuriating in the confidence and endurance you cultivate.

2. Find activities you enjoy: Embark on a quest of exploration, seeking exercises that stir your soul. Let your heart guide the way, whether it's the rhythmic beat of dancing, the meditative flow of yoga, or the refreshing surge of an aerobic adventure.

3. Establish a routine: Engrave exercise into your daily agenda, treating it as a sacred pact with yourself. **No negotiations, no excuses.** Carve out dedicated time for exercise, savoring it as an appointment that fuels your mental well-being.

4. Mix it up: Keep boredom at bay by infusing your exercise routine with a delightful medley of activities. Experiment, challenge yourself, and revel in the kaleidoscope of experiences. Your body and mind will prosper as they dance to the rhythm of novelty.

5. Mindful movement: Unveil the transformative power of exercise by approaching it through the lens of self-care and stress management. Immerse yourself fully in each movement, reveling in the sensations radiating through your body. Embrace exercise as a sanctuary where wellness and mental well-being unite.

A world brimming with serenity and calmness awaits those who grasp the transformative power of exercise as a tool to conquer depression. By appreciating the profound connection between exercise and anxiety reduction and integrating beneficial exercises into our lives, we forge a proactive path to mental health. Bask in releasing endorphins, reducing stress, increasing self-confidence, and the gift of rejuvenating sleep that exercise bestows. Allow aerobic activities, yoga, tai chi, dance, or mindful walking to guide you into the tranquil realm you crave.

SERENITY GATE MOTIVATION

CLOSING YOUR EYES, YOU step into a world beyond the realm of everyday pressures and stress. Your imagination awakens, painting vivid scenes that transport you to pure tranquility. Welcome to Serenity's Gate, a place of inner peace and relaxation.

As you step through the gate, you find yourself standing on the edge of a serene, crystal-clear beach. The water sparkles with a gentle shimmer, reflecting the vibrant colors of the surrounding foliage. Please take a moment to breathe in the crisp, clean air, feeling its refreshing essence fill your lungs and invigorate your spirit.

In the distance, you notice a small, handmade wooden boat waiting just for you. It beckons you with an open invitation. Stepping aboard, you feel the boat gently sway as you glide across the calm waters. Each stroke of the oars is met with a soft, melodic symphony, the song of serenity guiding you on your journey.

As you row deeper into the heart of the lake, the worries and stress of the outside world effortlessly melt away. The water beneath your fingertips carries away the weight of anxiety, leaving only a sense of calmness and peace. Take a moment to relish this sensation, allowing your body and mind to fully surrender to the soothing rhythm of the oars.

The surrounding landscape transforms into a vibrant pastel scene of colors and scents. Lush, green trees sway gently in the breeze, their leaves whispering secrets of tranquility. Fragrant flowers bloom beside the water's edge, releasing their captivating perfumes. The symphony of birdsong fills the air, harmonizing with the gentle lapping of water against the sides of the boat. The beauty surrounding you is a visual feast for the eyes and a balm for the soul. As you navigate the tranquil bay, notice how the tension in your muscles releases, your jaw unclenches, and your breathing becomes deep and rhythmic. Each stroke of the oars carries you further into a state of total relaxation, restoring balance and harmony within your being.

In the distance, you see a small, secluded island emerge. Its soft, sandy shores and shady palm trees promise a sanctuary of tranquility and renewal. Guiding the boat towards the shore, you disembark and allow your feet to sink into the warm sand, grounding you in the present moment.

Find a comfortable spot on the island, under the shade of a swaying palm tree, and make yourself comfortable. Close your eyes and feel the soothing warmth of the sun on your skin, melting away any lingering tension. As you breathe in the gentle, ocean-scented breeze, feel your worries carried away, leaving you with a sense of lightness and calm.

Now, imagine a gentle cascade of warm, golden light descending from above, enveloping your entire being. This radiant light, filled with healing energy, washes over you, healing any emotional or physical strain. It effortlessly unties the knots of anxiety and depression, replacing them with a sense of peace and contentment.

In this moment of stillness and bliss, allow yourself to embrace the tranquility surrounding you fully. Let go of any worries or doubts, surrendering to the healing powers of this place. Know that you are deserving of this respite and that you have the strength and capability to face whatever challenges may lie ahead.

As you begin to return to the present moment, bring with you the memory of Serenity's Gate. Allow it to serve as a reminder that within you lies a source of calm, a sanctuary from any troubling thought or worry. When the outside world becomes overwhelming, close your eyes and find solace in this visualization as you step through Serenity's Gate and reconnect with the peace that resides within you.

CHAPTER EIGHT

THE BENEFITS OF YOGA AS A PATH

TOWARD FREEDOM FROM ANXIETY AND DEPRESSION

Yoga is a way to freedom. By its constant practice, we can free ourselves from fear, anguish, and loneliness.

-Indra Devi

YOGA, AN ANCIENT PRACTICE that combines physical postures, breathing exercises, and meditation, is incredibly beneficial in managing anxiety and depression. In this chapter, we will discuss the specific benefits of **yoga** for stress relief and explore some powerful **yoga** positions that can help alleviate anxiety symptoms and diminish depression. By incorporating these practices into your routine, you can experience a **greater sense of calm, relaxation, and overall mental well-being.**

Deep Breathing Techniques:

One of the core principles of yoga is conscious breathing. Deep breathing techniques, such as **"*Ujjayi breath*"** or **"*Victorious breath*,"** focus on slowing down and extending the breath, activating the body's relaxation response. By bringing attention to the **present moment and connecting with the breath**, anxiety begins to fade away, and depression becomes a distant memory.

Grounding Poses:

Grounding poses, such as the "*Mountain Pose*":

Tadasana
(Mountain Pose)

Or *"Warrior Pose"*:

Virabhadrasana
(Warrior Pose)

The above poses help establish stability and security within the body. You can also add balance by practicing the ***"Tree Pose"***:

Vrksasana
(Tree Pose)

By rooting the feet into the ground, these poses help to release tension and bring a sense of calmness to the mind. As you hold these postures, imagine yourself as an **unshakable mountain**, firmly planted, free from the worries and stresses of life. Feel your feet becoming part of the floor, unmovable and unshakeable, from head to toe.

Heart-Opening Poses:

Depression can often cause us to hunch forward, experiencing a closed-off posture. **Heart-opening poses,** like the *"Bridge Pose"*:

Setubandha Sarvangasana
(Bridge Pose)

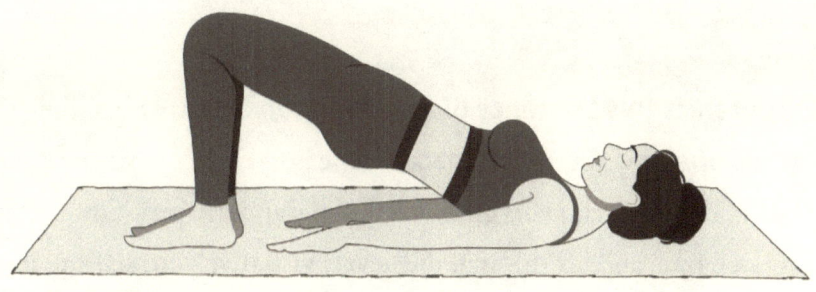

Or *"Camel Pose"*:

Ustrasana
(Camel Pose)

To counteract this tendency of hunching forward, try expanding the chest and **opening the heart space.** These poses help release any stored tension in the chest, allowing greater emotional and energetic flow. As you gently arch back and lift through the **heart, visualize yourself opening up to love, compassion, and self-acceptance while releasing fear or doubt.** Relax into these poses as much as possible, allowing your **heart to soften and release.**

Inversions:

Although inversions may appear challenging, they can be incredibly beneficial for anxiety relief. Poses such as *"Legs Up the Wall"*:

Viparita Karani
(Legs Up The Wall Pose)

Or *"Supported Shoulder Stand"*:

Sarvangasana
(Supported Shoulder Stand Pose)

They reverse blood flow and stimulate the parasympathetic nervous system, triggering a relaxation response. Inversions promote a shift in perspective by literally flipping us upside down. They release negative thought patterns, thereby helping depression and inviting a sense of calm and clarity. Stop and rest if you are feeling dizzy. Always **use your breath to deepen into the pose.**

The child's pose:

Also known as (*Balasana*) in yoga, it is a therapeutic and calming posture that can be beneficial for reducing anxiety. Here are a **few ways** in **which the child's pose can help alleviate stress and depression:**

Bālāsana
(Child's Pose)

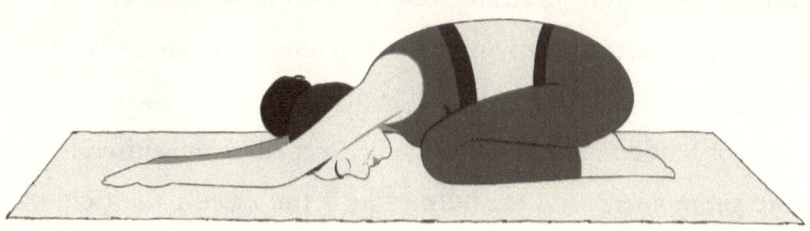

a). *Deep breathing:* In the child's pose, you are encouraged to take deep, slow breaths. This deep breathing activates the relaxation response in the body, triggering the **parasympathetic nervous system** and **reducing the physiological symptoms of anxiety,** such as rapid heartbeat and shallow breathing. Focusing on the breath can also help redirect attention away from anxious thoughts and bring a sense of calm.

b). *Encourages inward focus*: In the child's pose, your body is in a fetal position, which can create a sense of safety and security. This posture invites you to turn inward and focus on yourself rather than the external world. Directing attention inward and focusing on sensations in the body can cultivate a sense of grounding and present-moment awareness, which can help decrease depression.

c). *Releases tension*: Anxiety often manifests as physical tension in the body, particularly in the neck, shoulders, and back. The child's pose gently stretches and relaxes these areas, releasing physical tension and promoting relaxation. The elongation of the spine and the stretching of the hips can provide a sense of physical release and ease, reducing anxiety symptoms.

d). *Creates a sense of surrender*: The child's pose is often described as a resting and surrendering posture. By allowing your head to rest on the mat or a prop, you can create a sense of surrender and let go of any feelings of control or striving. This surrendering sensation can be particularly beneficial for individuals with depression, as it encourages a release of tension, facilitates a sense of acceptance and surrendering to the present moment, and can help reduce the need to anticipate or control future events.

e). *Cultivate mindful awareness*: The child's pose can be an opportunity to cultivate conscious awareness. While in the pose, you can bring your attention to the physical sensations, thoughts, and emotions that arise in the body. Observing these experiences with curiosity and non-judgment allows you to better understand your stressful triggers and how your body and mind respond to them. This increased self-aware-ness can help manage anxiety and depression and make conscious choices to reduce their impact on your well-being.

It's worth noting that some yoga poses may only be suitable for more experienced practitioners, so depending on your physical limitations or personal preferences, proceed at your own pace. If you are new to yoga or have any physical concerns, it's advisable to practice under the guidance of a qualified yoga instructor to ensure proper alignment and modification. Plus, its a great place to have fun and meet people, not to mention the benefits of a slender fit body.

Shavasana
(Resting Pose)

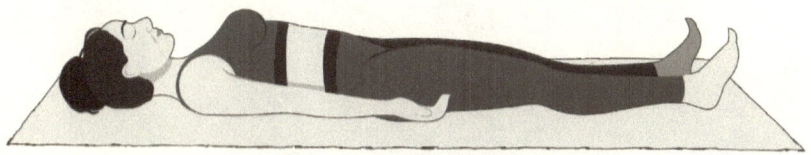

Shavasana is the final relaxation pose in yoga, where you lie comfortably on your back, completely surrendering to the present moment. As you melt into the ground, this pose induces a deep state of relaxation and allows the body and mind to integrate the benefits of your yoga practice. Shavasana promotes a sense of deep release, offering a temporary respite from the constant worrying mind. It is a reminder that sometimes, the best way to manage depression is through **surrendering and letting go into enjoying the moment.** Take a quick scan from your head to your toes, then completely let go, **embracing total relaxation.**

Incorporating yoga into your daily routine can be a powerful tool for managing anxiety. The **breathing techniques, grounding poses, heart-opening poses, inversions, and Shavasana** all work together to nourish your **mind-body and spirit**. By consistently practicing these yoga positions and techniques, you can cultivate a greater sense of calm, inner strength, and resilience in the face of anxiety and depression. Remember, yoga is **a journey, allowing you to be gentle with yourself** and embrace the transformative power of this ancient practice.

Yoga Lake Serenity

CLOSE YOUR EYES AND imagine yourself in a place of Pure Serenity, where time slows and the world's worries melt away. You find yourself standing at the edge of a quiet lake, surrounded by lush greenery and towering trees. The air around you is crisp and clean, carrying the gentle scent of flowers and earth.

As you take a deep breath, you notice the soft sound of birds chirping and the distant rustling of leaves in the breeze. The sun's golden rays filter through the branches, glowing warmly upon the peaceful space before you. You have come to practice your yoga in this enchanting setting. With each deliberate step, your bare feet connect with the coolness of the earth beneath you. You find a perfect spot on a patch of soft grass overlooking the lake's sparkling waters. As you settle into your mat, you savor the sensation of the ground supporting your body, grounding you in this present moment.

Gently closing your eyes, you bring awareness to your breath, feeling the air flowing in and out of your body. With each inhale, you draw in the tranquility of this serene setting, and with each exhale, you release any tension or stress. The rhythm of your breath becomes a soothing melody, guiding you deeper into the stillness within.

As you open your eyes, your gaze is met by the breathtaking beauty surrounding you. The branches of the trees sway gently in response to the wind's whispered touch, creating a dance of ever-changing shadows on the ground. The sunlight filters through and makes a radiant pattern of warm hues on the lake's surface, as if nature is painting a masterpiece just for you.

You begin to move through your yoga practice, each pose an effortless extension of your body and spirit. With arms outstretched, you embody the grace and strength of a majestic tree, the roots of your being sinking deep into the earth. You flow through flowing sun salutations, feeling the warmth of the sun energizing every cell within you.

As you move into standing poses, you become aware of the firm and steady connection you have forged with the earth beneath you, finding stability and balance in each pose—the air brushes against your skin, carrying a sense of freedom and expansion. Your body becomes a vessel for the energy of this serene setting, flowing effortlessly from one pose to the next.

In seated and reclined poses, you surrender entirely to the support of the ground, allowing yourself to melt into its embrace. The sounds of nature become a gentle symphony, guiding your practice and deepening your sense of peace. You tune into the songs of the birds, feeling a harmonious connection between your breath, your body, and the world around you.

As your practice comes to a close, you find yourself lying flat on your mat, basking in the stillness and tranquility surrounding you. The gentle lapping of the lake's waters and the rustling of leaves create a soothing lullaby, inviting you to rest, restore, and rejuvenate.

A profound sense of calm and inner stillness washes over you as you slowly rise from your final relaxation. You feel deep gratitude for this beautiful, serene setting, for the practice of yoga that nourishes your body and spirit, and for the opportunity to experience this moment of pure bliss.

Carry this visualization with you, allowing it to inspire your future practices and reminding you of the profound connection between your yoga practice and the natural world. May you always find peace and harmony within the sanctuary of your yoga practice, and may the beauty of the world around you forever guide and uplift your spirit.

CHAPTER NINE

MASSAGE THE HEALING TOUCH

MASSAGE AS A TREATMENT MODALITY FOR ANXIETY AND DEPRESSION

Take care of your body, it's the only place you have to live. -Jim Rohn

IN THIS CRAZY WORLD we live in today, anxiety and depression have become an all-too-common reaction for many. The pressures of modern life and the constant barrage of stressors can take a toll on our mental and emotional well-being. Consequently, individuals suffering from stress fervently seek natural and holistic approaches to alleviate their symptoms. Among these, massage therapy has emerged as a powerful modality in combating anxiety and alleviating depression, providing a haven of relaxation and healing. In this chapter, we investigate the rich history of massage therapy, explore the various massage modalities, and shed light on its remarkable benefits in holistic healing.

Section 1: A Historical Perspective:

The roots of massage therapy can be traced back to ancient civilizations, where the healing power of touch was revered. In **Ancient China,** texts dating back over **4,000 years** describe massage techniques as crucial to medical practices. Similarly, the **Egyptians, Greeks, and Romans** utilized massage to promote healing, rejuvenation, and overall wellness.

During the Middle Ages, massage therapy fell into obscurity as societal norms influenced perceptions of touch. However, in the **19th century,** the work of **Swedish physician Per Henrik Ling** revived interest in massage therapy. His system, known as Swedish massage, became a cornerstone of modern massage practice, emphasizing long, flowing strokes and kneading techniques to promote relaxation and physical well-being.

Since then, massage therapy has evolved and diversified, with various modalities emerging to cater to specific needs and goals. Let us explore some of these modalities and their unique benefits in addressing anxiety and depression.

Modalities and their Benefits:

Swedish massage:

The most widely practiced modality lies at the heart of massage therapy. This technique employs a combination of **long, gliding strokes, kneading, and rhythmic tapping to ease muscle tension,**

improve circulation, and induce relaxation. The benefits of Swedish massage extend beyond the physical realm, reaching deep into the **emotional and mental spheres.**

Research studies have shown that Swedish massage can reduce stress hormones, such as cortisol, while simultaneously increasing serotonin and dopamine levels, the neurotransmitters associated with happiness and relaxation. These physiological changes help quiet the mind, promote a sense of calm, and alleviate symptoms of anxiety and depression.

Moreover, a Swedish massage session's nurturing touch and soothing atmosphere create a therapeutic space that invites deep relaxation, often leading to a meditative state. This state of mindfulness can help individuals experiencing depression detach from their worries and enter a state of inner peace and tranquility.

Deep Tissue Massage:

While Swedish massage focuses on relaxation and overall well-being, **deep tissue massage** is tailored to **address specific muscular concerns** and release tension held deep within the body. This modality utilizes slow, targeted pressure to reach the deeper muscle and connective tissue layers.

The benefits of deep tissue massage in the treatment of anxiety lie in the release of muscle tension and the subsequent reduction of physical discomfort. Chronic muscle tension is often associated with anxiety, exacerbating symptoms and creating a stress feedback loop. By addressing these muscular imbalances, deep-tissue massage can alleviate physical discomfort, creating relief and relaxation. Moreover, the intensity of deep tissue massage triggers the release of endorphins, the body's natural painkillers and mood elevators. These induce a sense of euphoria and well-being, also helping to mitigate symptoms of depression and promote a general understanding of calm.

Aromatherapy massage:

Combines the power of touch with the therapeutic properties of essential oils extracted from plants. This modality harnesses the profound effects of scent on the **limbic system,** the part of the brain responsible for emotions and memories. Different essential oils possess distinct therapeutic properties that can be tailored to address specific stress-reducing properties. Lavender essential oil, for instance, is known for its calming and soothing effects, while citrus oils, such as bergamot and orange, are prized for their uplifting and energizing properties.

During an aromatherapy massage session, the therapist incorporates these **essential oils** into the massage oil or lotion. As the client inhales the delightful aromas, the body absorbs the oils through the skin, initiating a cascade of therapeutic benefits. The scent receptors in the nasal passages send signals to the brain, **triggering the release of endorphins, reducing stress hormone levels, and promoting deep relaxation.**

Additionally, inhaling these soothing fragrances can stimulate the release of **serotonin and dopamine,** the neurotransmitters associated with elevated mood and reduced anxiety. The synergy between touch and scent creates a powerful healing experience, allowing for a profound release of tension in both the body and mind.

Thai Massage:

Thai massage is an ancient healing modality combining acupressure, stretching, and yoga-like positions in Thailand. This unique approach focuses on restoring harmony and balance within the body by stimulating the flow of vital energy, known as "**Sen,**" through specific energy lines.

Thai massage offers several benefits that can be particularly helpful for individuals experiencing anxiety. Firstly, the assisted stretching techniques in Thai massage improve flexibility, promote better posture, and release physical tension. These material changes can profoundly impact one's emotional state and can contribute to a reduction in depression.

Moreover, Thai massage incorporates acupressure on specific points along the energy lines, similar to **acupuncture.** These pressure points, when stimulated, release stagnant energy and promote a balanced flow throughout the body, creating a sense of relaxation and well-being. Thai massage sessions are often conducted in a meditative, serene atmosphere, with gentle music and dim lighting. This ambiance, coupled with rhythmic movements and nurturing touch, creates a safe space for individuals to release tension, quiet their racing thoughts, and experience a profound sense of calm and tranquility.

Acupressure:

It is a massage modality that involves applying pressure to specific points on the body to stimulate healing and promote overall well-being. Originating from **traditional Chinese medicine (TCM)**, it is based on the belief that the body has energetic pathways, known as **meridians**, through which **life force energy**, also known as **qi (chee),** flows.

When it comes to the management of anxiety and depression, **acupressure** can be a powerful tool to help alleviate symptoms and promote relaxation. By targeting **specific acupoints, acupressure** can help release tension, reduce stress levels, and restore the **balance of energy** within the body.

One of the primary acupoints that can be beneficial for anxiety and depression is known as the **"Yintang" or "Third Eye" point.** Located **between the eyebrows,** this point is believed to calm the mind, relieve stress, and promote mental clarity. Gently applying pressure to this point can help soothe anxiety, ease mental restlessness, and promote a **sense of calmness.**

Another acupoint that can be effective for managing anxiety and depression is the **"Shenmen" point.** It is located on the ear and is also known as the **"Spirit Gate."** Stimulating this point can help reduce stress, promote relaxation, and enhance overall well-being. **Massaging** the **Shenmen point** can have a calming effect on the mind and may help alleviate symptoms of anxiety and depression.

The "Neiguan" or "Inner Gate" point is another **acupoint** commonly used to address anxiety and depression. It is located on the inner wrist, about three finger-widths above the crease. Applying pressure or massaging this point can help relieve emotional stress, reduce anxiety, and promote a sense of inner calmness.

In addition to these **acupoints,** several others may be utilized based on an individual's specific symptoms and needs. These include the **"Taixi"**

or **"Kidney 3" point,** located in the inner ankle depression, which is believed to tonify the kidneys and promote emotional stability, and the **"Sanyinjiao" or "Spleen 6" point**, located inside the leg above the ankle bone, which can help regulate emotions and relieve anxiety.

- **Pericardium 6 (P6)**: Located on the inside of the inner arm, approximately three finger-widths from the wrist crease between the two tendons every body is different with practice you will find your sweet spot. Stimulating this point is believed to help calm the mind and relieve anxiety.

- **Heart 7 (HT7)**: Found on the inner hand at the crease in your wrist, in line with the little finger. This point is thought to help balance emotions and calm the mind.

- **Governing Vessel 24.5 (GV24.5):** This is located between the eyebrows and the third eye in the indentation where the bridge of the nose and the forehead meet. Stimulating this point is believed to help relieve anxiety and promote relaxation.

- **Conception Vessel 17 (CV17)** is located above the diaphragm at the center of the breastbone. Gently pressing this point is thought to help alleviate emotional distress and promote a sense of calm.

- **Stomach 36 (ST36)**: This point is situated on the inside of the lower leg, about four finger-widths below the knee, on the outside of the ankle. It is believed to promote overall well-being and help relieve stress and depression symptoms.

It is important to note that while **acupressure** can be beneficial for managing anxiety and depression, it should not replace professional medical treatment or therapy. It can be used as a complementary therapy to support overall well-being and aid in relaxation. If you are experiencing severe anxiety or depression, it is crucial to seek guidance from a healthcare professional.

When performing acupressure on oneself or receiving it from a trained practitioner, it is important to apply moderate pressure and adjust it to your comfort level. Deep, slow breaths and a calming environment can enhance the effects of acupressure and promote relaxation.

In conclusion, acupressure is a massage modality that can provide relief from anxiety and depression. By targeting specific **acupoints** on the body, **acupressure** can help restore balance, release tension, and promote a sense of well-being. While it can be a valuable tool in managing these conditions, consulting with a qualified healthcare professional is essential to ensure a comprehensive treatment approach.

Through the ages, massage therapy has played an integral role in healing and promoting wellness. In treating anxiety and depression, **massage** offers a gentle yet powerful approach that utilizes touch, scent, and relaxation techniques to soothe the body and mind. The various massage modalities discussed in this chapter, including **Swedish, Deep Tissue, Aromatherapy, Thai, and Acupressure**, offer unique benefits that can alleviate anxiety symptoms, promote relaxation, and foster a sense of overall well-being. While **massage therapy** is not a substitute for professional mental health treatment for severe anxiety and depression disorders, it can be a valuable complementary tool, providing individuals with a safe and nurturing space to unwind, release tension, and experience emotional healing.

In the following chapters, we will explore additional complementary approaches to anxiety treatment and depression relief that can be combined with massage therapy, allowing for a **holistic** and multifaceted approach toward healing the **mind-body and spirit.**

HAVEN OF SERENITY

IN A SECLUDED VALLEY, nestled between mist-covered mountains and lush green forests, lies a hidden sanctuary known as the Haven of Serenity. A place where tranquility and healing intertwine, offering respite to those seeking comfort from the world's troubles.

As you walk the moss-covered paths, the air becomes infused with the intoxicating aroma of wildflowers and the gentle gurgle of a nearby stream. Dappled sunlight filters through the canopy of ancient trees, casting a warm glow upon the path ahead.

Ascending stone steps, you arrive at a serene clearing adorned with vibrant blossoms and soothing water features. The air here seems to hum with soothing energy as if the very essence of tranquility has settled upon this sacred space.

A grand wooden pavilion awaits in the center of the clearing, its ornately carved pillars and soft cushions inviting you to surrender to a moment of pause and reflection. As you step inside, a gentle breeze carries with it the faint scent of essential oils and the distant sound of birdsong, enveloping you in a cocoon of relaxation.

Before you relax and settle in, you notice an intricately woven carpet depicting a lush meadow where flowers sway in a gentle breeze, their vibrant hues dancing in harmony with the sun's golden rays. As you sit on one of the plush cushions, the patterns in the carpet become animated, offering a glimpse into a world where anxieties are gently carried away on a gentle current.

As you close your eyes and settle into the soft cushions, you take a deep breath, allowing the fresh mountain air to fill your lungs. With each exhale, you release tension and worries, feeling a weight lift from your shoulders and a softening of the muscles.

With a gentle touch, your fingertips wander to your temples, massaging tiny circles in a comforting rhythm. As your touch lulls your mind into a state of relaxation, the swirling pattern in front of you shifts, revealing a serene, meandering river, its banks lined with vibrant wildflowers.

A soft, melodic stream weaves through the forest, inviting you to immerse your feet in its cool embrace. And so, you dip your toes into the crystal-clear water, feeling its gentle caress wash away residual anxieties.

As your fingers trace the path along your jawline, your breath deepens, calming the racing thoughts that once occupied your mind. The river responds, revealing a majestic waterfall cascading from a towering cliff into a serene pool below. The rushing water fills your ears, soothing your senses and relieving any remaining tension.

Your hands find their way to your neck, massaging away the layers of stress that have settled there. As your touch awakens a sense of release, the stream meanders and unfolds into a breathtaking forest scene. Towering trees stand as guardians, their branches dancing to the rhythm of a gentle breeze.

You take a deep breath, inhaling the earthy scent of moss and leaves, letting it ground you in the present moment. The touch of the massage transforms into the gentle rustling of leaves as if the forest itself is reaching out to envelop you in its healing embrace.

Moving your hands to your shoulders, you knead away the tight knots formed from the world's weight. As the tension melts away, the bubbling brook reveals a serene mountaintop, where you stand with arms outstretched, feeling a sense of strength and empowerment radiating from within.

Closing your eyes, you feel the cool, crisp air brush against your skin, cleansing away any lingering doubts. With each breath, you draw in clarity and exhale any traces of remaining anxiety.

Continuing, your hands explore your arms and hands, tenderly massaging away the strain and tension carried in these often-overlooked parts of your body. The stream bends and unfolds into a peaceful garden, where delicate butterflies flit from flower to flower, their graceful movements reflecting the lightness and freedom you now feel.

You release a contented sigh as you immerse yourself in the garden's beauty, feeling a newfound connection to the present moment and an appreciation for the simple joys surrounding you.

As your hands guide your touch toward your chest and abdomen, you breathe deeply, filling your lungs with nourishing oxygen and exhaling any remnants of anxiety or stress. The garden transforms into a serene meadow, where a gentle breeze sways the tall grasses, creating a soothing symphony.

With each inhalation, you envision drawing in tranquility; with each exhale, you release any unease or doubt. Your breath becomes a lifeline, anchoring you to the present and reminding you of your inherent ability to find calm within.

Moving your hands to your legs and feet, you massage away any residual tension, allowing your muscles to surrender to the soothing touch. The meadow reveals a mountaintop view, where the sun sets in a blaze of colors, casting a golden glow over the world.

As you gaze at this awe-inspiring sight, you feel deep gratitude for the journey you have embarked upon and the obstacles you have overcome. Your anxieties dissipate with each breath and touch, replaced by a renewed sense of clarity and inner peace.

As the visualization comes to a close, you open your eyes, feeling refreshed and rejuvenated by this journey of relaxation and self-discovery. The Haven of Serenity has given you a precious gift—a reminder of your strength and resilience and a deeper understanding of the power within. Allow your eyes to softly close again as you continue down your enchanted path.

Leaving the Haven of Serenity, you carry the tranquility of this sacred space with you, allowing it to guide you through whatever challenges may lie ahead. The natural surroundings, the gentle touch, and the rhythmic breath are powerful tools for managing anxiety and finding inner peace.

With this newfound knowledge, you step back onto the path, ready to face the world with a renewed sense of calm and resilience. The tranquility of the Haven of Serenity will forever remain within you, a beacon of serenity to draw upon whenever anxiety threatens to cloud your spirit. As you continue down the path from the Haven of Serenity, you can't help but feel a sense of lightness and clarity that envelops your being. The world's weight no longer feels as heavy on your shoulders, and the worries that once plagued your mind seem distant and insignificant in the grand scheme. The path winds through the enchanting forest, with sunlight filtering through the dense canopy above, creating a mesmerizing play of light and shadow on the forest floor. The air feels crisp and rejuvenating, carrying the faint scent of wildflowers and earth.

As you walk, you notice the sound of gentle rustling overhead, and you look up to see a family of squirrels playfully scampering along the branches. Their joyful antics bring a smile to your face and remind you of life's simple pleasures.

Following the path, you come across a small, secluded clearing bathed in soft sunshine. A serene pond rests at the center, its surface smooth as glass, reflecting the surrounding trees and sky. The water shimmers with an ethereal beauty, beckoning you to come closer and experience its calming embrace.

You approach the pond's edge, feeling a gentle breeze brush against your skin. Closing your eyes, you take a deep breath, inhaling the purity of the moment. As you exhale, the tension and worries that may still linger within you are carried away by the wind, leaving you feeling lighter and more at peace.

Curious, you dip your fingers into the cool water, feeling its gentle caress against your skin. The ripples that form ripple across your own being, soothing any residual anxieties and creating a sense of harmony.

You sit by the water's edge, listening to the gentle sounds of nature that surround you. The melodic chirping of birds fills the air as if nature is serenading you, inviting you to let go of any remaining tension and immerse yourself in the present moment.

As you bask in the tranquility of the pond, you notice a group of delicate lotus flowers gracefully floating on the surface. Their vibrant colors and elegant petals symbolize purity, enlightenment, and spiritual awakening.

You watch as a butterfly lands delicately on one of the lotus flowers, its wings shimmering with hues of the rainbow. The sight fills you with a sense of awe and wonder, reminding you of the interconnectedness of all living beings and the beauty that can be found in even the smallest moments. Feeling inspired, you take a moment to meditate by the pond. Closing your eyes, you focus on your breath, allowing your inhales and exhales to merge with the natural rhythm of the world around you.

With each breath, you visualize the worries and anxieties of the outside world drifting away, leaving a sense of calm and clarity in their wake. You feel grounded, rooted to the very essence of the earth, and connected to a more significant source of peace and tranquility.

As you open your eyes, a deep gratitude washes over you. You are grateful for the moments of stillness and serenity you found within the Haven of Serenity and for the reminders that nature offers of the resilience and beauty within you.

Leaving the peaceful pond behind, you continue on your journey, carrying the tranquility and calmness of the Haven of Serenity within your heart. The path ahead may still be filled with challenges, but you know that you hold the power to navigate them with grace and poise.

You walk on with a newfound sense of strength and inner peace, guided by the lessons and serenity you discovered within the hidden haven. As you venture forth, you intend to infuse every step with mindfulness, embracing the present moment and allowing tranquility to be a constant companion on your journey.

Chapter Ten

The Ancient Art of Acupuncture

Harnessing the Body's Energy for Anxiety and Depression Relief

The greatest medicine of all is to teach people how not to need it.-Hippocrates

ACUPUNCTURE, AN ANCIENT HEALING practice rooted in Chinese medicine, has captivated the curiosity and interest of people worldwide. With its origins dating back over 3,000 years, acupuncture is a holistic approach that seeks to restore balance and harmony within the body by stimulating specific points along the body's energy pathways. In this chapter, we embark on a journey through the rich history of acupuncture, explore the principles behind its effectiveness, and understand its remarkable benefits in alleviating anxiety and reducing depression.

A Historical Perspective:

The ancient history of acupuncture can be traced back to ancient China, where it was developed as a vital component of **Traditional Chinese Medicine (TCM).** The earliest written documentation of acupuncture can be found in the ancient Chinese medical text known as the **Huangdi Neijing,** or **The Yellow Emperor's Inner Canon,** dating back to around 200 BCE. This influential text outlines the theories and practices of Chinese medicine, including acupuncture, anatomy, pathologies, and the concept of **qi (pronounced "chee").** This vital life force flows within the body.

Over the centuries, acupuncture evolved and became increasingly sophisticated. During the **Han Dynasty** (206 BCE - 220 CE), a comprehensive text called the **Nanjing, or Classic of Difficult Issues,** was written, providing further insights into the theory and techniques of acupuncture. The development of acupuncture continued, with new schools of thought emerging and refining the practice throughout the following dynasties.

In the 17th century, acupuncture faced a significant challenge as Western medicine gained prominence in China. However, the practice continued to be passed down through generations in secret and was eventually recognized and integrated into mainstream medicine in the mid-20th century. Today, acupuncture is widely practiced and recognized as a valuable complementary therapy for various health conditions, including anxiety and depression.

The Principles and Techniques of Acupuncture:

At the core of acupuncture philosophy is the concept of **qi**, the vital life force that flows through distinct pathways in the body called meridians. According to **TCM,** when the flow of **qi** is balanced and unobstructed, the body is in a state of health. However, when **qi** becomes imbalanced or blocked, it can lead to pain, illness, and emotional imbalances, including anxiety.

In order to restore the flow of qi and bring about healing, acupuncture employs the insertion of fine, sterile needles into specific points along the **body's meridians.** These points, known as acupoints, are carefully selected based on the individual's unique symptoms and constitution. The sensation experienced during acupuncture varies from person to person but is often described as a mild tingling or dull ache.

Acupuncture techniques may include additional modalities such as **cupping, moxibustion** (the burning of **mugwort herb** near acupoints), and **electroacupuncture** (using a mild electric current). These techniques complement the acupuncture treatment, further stimulating the body's energy flow and promoting healing.

Benefits of Regulating the Nervous System for Anxiety and Depression Relief:

Anxiety disorders and depression symptoms can disrupt the delicate balance of the nervous system, resulting in heightened apprehension, worry, and stress. Acupuncture offers a unique way to regulate the autonomic nervous system, which governs the body's automatic responses, such as heart rate, digestion, and breathing.

Studies have shown that acupuncture can modulate the autonomic nervous system's **sympathetic (fight-or-flight) and parasympathetic (rest-and-digest) branches**. By stimulating specific acupoints, acupuncture can activate the parasympathetic branch, inducing a state of deep relaxation and reducing anxiety symptoms.

Endorphins are our body's natural painkillers and mood enhancers. They play a vital role in reducing depression and promoting well-being. Acupuncture can stimulate the release of endorphins, creating a natural high and promoting a sense of calm and relaxation.

Endorphin Release:

The insertion of acupuncture needles into specific acupoints triggers the release of endorphins, which reduce physical pain and help alleviate anxiety symptoms. These endorphins flood the body, promoting a sense of euphoria and acting as an effective natural remedy for depression.

Stress Reduction:

Chronic stress is a significant contributing factor to anxiety disorders and depression symptoms. Acupuncture can lower stress hormone levels, such as cortisol, in the body, effectively reducing the physiological stress response. Through its ability to regulate the body's stress response, acupuncture can help individuals experience decreased tension and promote a greater sense of calmness. By disrupting the negative feedback loop of stress and anxiety, acupuncture offers a valuable tool for managing the symptoms of anxiety disorders and depression.

Emotional Balance:

Acupuncture aims to restore balance within the body, not only on a physical level but also on an emotional level. In **TCM**, emotions are considered an integral part of overall health, and imbalances in emotions can manifest as physical symptoms.

By restoring the flow of qi and harmonizing the body's energy, **acupuncture** can help rebalance emotions, soothe anxiety, and promote emotional well-being. Regular acupuncture treatments can help individuals better understand their emotional states and build resilience in managing depression.

From its ancient origins to its integration into modern healthcare, acupuncture continues to captivate and enthrall with its holistic approach to healing. The principles and techniques of acupuncture, rooted in the concept of **qi** and **meridians,** provide a unique avenue for addressing anxiety and promoting overall well-being.

The benefits of acupuncture for depression relief are wide-ranging, from regulating the nervous system and promoting relaxation to stimulating the release of endorphins and reducing stress levels. By restoring balance within the body, acupuncture creates a pathway toward emotional healing, equipping individuals with a tool to navigate the challenges of anxiety with greater resilience and serenity.

Chinese Palace Gardens

IMAGINE YOURSELF STANDING IN front of majestic red and gold gates, the entrance to an enchanting ancient Chinese Palace. These gates exude a sense of awe and wonder, inviting you to enter a world of serenity and beauty. As you pass through the gates, you are greeted by an expansive courtyard, alive with the vibrant colors of meticulously manicured bonsai trees and blooming flowers. The fragrance of nature's abundance perfumes the air, infusing you with tranquility.

In this courtyard, you come across a wise elderly figure dressed in flowing robes of traditional Chinese attire. His eyes radiate empathy and understanding, and you feel an instant connection as his eyes warmly beckon you to follow him along a meandering stone path. With every step, a wave of calm washes over you, and you realize that you are not alone in your journey through anxiety. The presence of this wise elder provides comfort and reassurance, assuring you that there is guidance and support along your path.

Leaving the courtyard, you find yourself immersed in the palace gardens, a sanctuary of nature's embrace. Majestic trees stretch upwards, their branches whispering ancient secrets passed down through generations. The gentle rustling of leaves and the melodic cascade of water from stone fountains create a harmonious chime, soothing your spirit and melting away your worries.

As you explore the gardens, you stumble upon a shimmering koi pond, its surface reflecting the vibrant hues of the surrounding flora. A delicate wooden bridge spans the pond, inviting you to cross over into a deeper connection with your subconscious mind. With each step, you release the weight of anxiety, feeling the cleansing touch of nature's embrace as it washes away your worries. The bridge becomes a symbolic pathway between the conscious and subconscious, allowing you to let go of stresses and fears that no longer serve you.

Continuing your journey, you enter an ornately gilded chamber adorned with glistening mirrors, each reflecting not only your physical appearance but also your inner emotions. As you approach, you notice a flicker of doubt and anxiety in your reflection. However, as you gaze more profoundly, the reflection transforms, revealing a glimmer of resilience and strength. This chamber is a Palace of Reflection—a space where introspection and self-acceptance lead to personal growth.

An ethereal figure materializes within this chamber, embodying inner peace and acceptance. They share ancient wisdom, teaching you the art of self-compassion and finding solace in the present moment. Encouraging you to acknowledge your fears and emotions with compassion guides you toward self-awareness and self-acceptance. In the reflection of the mirrors, you learn to embrace your strengths and nurture your vulnerabilities, recognizing that anxiety is a part of your journey but does not define you.

Leaving the Chamber of Reflection, you ascend a grand staircase leading to the Hall of Resilience. The hall is bathed in a warm golden light emanating from elegant lanterns suspended from the ceiling. Like stars in the night sky, they illuminate the walls adorned with murals depicting tales of triumph over adversity. Each mural showcases the unwavering courage and resilience of those who faced their fears head-on. As you admire these stories of triumph, you realize that anxiety, though powerful, can be met with resilience and strength.

At the center of the hall stands a majestic golden dragon, its fierce gaze capturing your attention. You gaze back unafraid. The dragon symbolizes the embodiment of ancient wisdom and inner power. Its scales glimmer, and its eyes sparkle with otherworldly energy that resonates with your own inner strength.

Approaching the dragon, you feel its presence, calming your racing heart and easing the knots in your stomach. As you stand beside this majestic creature, it invites you to touch its shimmering scales. As your hand grazes its surface, a surge of energy courses through your veins, filling you with a newfound sense of resilience and courage.

In the dragon's presence, you realize that anxiety is not a foe to be fought against or suppressed. Instead, it is a force that can be harnessed and transformed into fuel for personal growth. The dragon imparts its wisdom, guiding you to embrace your anxieties as catalysts for transformation and stepping stones toward becoming the best version of yourself.

Leaving the Hall of Resilience, you find yourself in a serene court-yard bathed in the soft glow of lanterns and adorned with delicate cherry blossom trees. The blossoms, with their delicate petals, sym-bolize the transient nature of life and the beauty that can be found in embracing impermanence.

As you walk beneath the blossoms, their delicate fragrance wafts through the air, whispering ancient teachings about acceptance and letting go. Each step becomes a meditation, allowing you to release any attachment to worries and anxieties that no longer serve you. Now, you understand that anxiety is not an enemy to be conquered but rather a teacher, guiding you toward a deeper understanding of yourself and the world around you.

At the center of the courtyard, you discover a grand Meditation Pavilion, its intricately carved pillars and soft cushions beckoning you to find solace within its walls. Stepping inside, you are en-veloped by a serene atmosphere; the gentle flickering of candlelight and the soothing sound of flowing water bring peace to your soul.

Sitting on one of the cushions, you close your eyes and let the stillness wash over you. In this tranquil space, you connect with the depths of your being, tapping into a wellspring of inner peace and calm. As you breathe in deeply, you envision inhaling pure serenity and exhaling all traces of anxiety, feeling lighter with each breath.

As the moments pass, you find yourself in a state of deep relaxation, your mind attuned to the present moment. In this peaceful state, you realize that anxiety is not a permanent state of being but rather a passing wave in the grand ocean of life. As the tides rise and fall, so does anxiety ebb and flow.

With this newfound wisdom and the tranquil energy of this sacred space, you step out of the pavilion and find yourself back at the palace entrance. As you gaze upon the magnificent red and gold gates, you feel a sense of gratitude for the journey you have taken within.

Leaving the palace, you carry the teachings and experiences gained along the way. The image of the wise elder, the tranquility of the garden, the reflections in the Chamber of Reflection, the resilience of the Hall of Resilience, and the peace found in the Meditation Pavilion become touchstones of inner strength and serenity that you can revisit in moments of anxiety.

As you step through the gates and back into the world outside, you carry the essence of the palace within you. The wisdom, resilience, and peace you discover within its walls are a guiding light, empowering you to navigate life's challenges with grace and a newfound sense of calm.

CHAPTER ELEVEN

HEALING POWER OF HYDROTHERAPY

SOOTHING DEPRESSION AND ANXIETY

You can't stop the waves, but you can learn to surf. -Jon Kabat-Zinn

IN THIS CHAPTER, WE will dive into the world of **hydrotherapy** and explore its transformative potential in managing anxiety and dissipating Depression. **Hydrotherapy**, a therapeutic approach that utilizes water in various forms, has been used for centuries to promote physical, mental, and emotional well-being. In the context of anxiety, **hydrotherapy** offers a gentle and soothing antidote to the overwhelming stress and tension that often accompanies this condition. By immersing ourselves in water and engaging in **hydrotherapeutic practices,** we can find a calming refuge from Depression that helps us regain balance and tranquility.

Understanding Hydrotherapy:

Hydrotherapy uses water to heal, harnessing its unique qualities to enhance wellness. From ancient civilizations to modern scientific research, the therapeutic benefits of water have been widely acknowledged. **Hydrotherapy** provides a holistic approach to relaxation, rejuvenation, and stress relief, whether through bathing, soaking, or using hydro-massage techniques.

The Role of Hydrotherapy in Anxiety and Depression:

Anxiety and Depression often manifest as muscle tension, restlessness, and an overactive mind. **Hydrotherapy** addresses these symptoms by creating a soothing and nurturing environment for the body and mind. Water's ability to support weightlessness allows for a release of physical tension, while its calming properties help to quiet the mind and promote relaxation. By immersing ourselves in the healing embrace of water, we can embark on a self-care and anxiety-reduction journey. Allowing the warm embrace of soothing waters can help reduce symptoms of depression and lead to a general feeling of well-being.

Benefits of Hydrotherapy for Anxiety and Depression:

Incorporating hydrotherapy into our stress-management practice can yield a wide range of benefits, including:

1. **Physical relaxation**: Warm water relaxes and loosens tense muscles, reducing physical symptoms of anxiety such as tightness and pain.

2. **Mental calmness**: Immersing oneself in water provides tranquility and helps quiet a racing mind, offering respite from anxious thoughts and worries.

3. **Stress reduction:** Hydrotherapy stimulates the release of endorphins, natural mood-boosting chemicals in the brain, reducing stress and improving overall well-being.

4. **Improved sleep:** Hydrotherapy before bed can promote better-quality sleep, allowing for deeper rest and enhanced recovery from anxiety challenges.

5. **Emotional release:** Water has a unique ability to facilitate emotional release, creating a space for gentle catharsis and offering solace during times of heightened emotional turbulence.

Hydrotherapy Techniques for Anxiety and Depression:

Here are a few hydrotherapy techniques that can be incorporated into your stress-management routine:

1. **Warm Baths:** Soak in a warm bath, adding essential oils or bath salts known for their calming properties, such as lavender or chamomile. Allow yourself to fully relax and let go of tension as you immerse yourself in the warm water.

2. **Hydro-Massage:** Explore hydro-massage techniques, such as using a handheld showerhead or massaging jets in a pool or spa. Focus on areas of tension and allow the rhythmic water flow to alleviate muscle soreness and promote relaxation.

3. Cold Water Therapy: Brief exposure to cold water, such as a cool shower, can stimulate the body's natural relaxation response and provide calmness and mental clarity.

4. Water Meditation: Practice mindfulness meditation while submerged in water. Close your eyes, focus on holding your breath, and allow the water to carry away any anxious thoughts or tension.

5. Saunas have a rich history dating back thousands of years and have been used across various cultures for their therapeutic benefits. The ancient Finns, for instance, are renowned for their sauna tradition, which they have practiced for over 2,000 years. Initially used for bathing and religious ceremonies, saunas gradually became recognized for their profound physical and mental benefits. The heat and steam in saunas and jacuzzis induce a range of physiological responses in the body, including increased blood circulation and heart rate, which promote relaxation and an overall sense of well-being. The warmth helps to relax muscles, relieve tension, and promote the release of endorphins, which are natural mood-boosting neurotransmitters. Additionally, the sweating process that occurs in saunas aids in detoxification by flushing out toxins and impurities from the body. This ancient practice has stood the test of time, offering a natural and effective way to alleviate anxiety and promote relaxation.

Hydrotherapy is a powerful tool in the management of anxiety, offering a unique and refreshing approach to finding peace and relaxation. By immersing ourselves in the **healing embrace of water,** we can tap into its soothing properties and experience a profound release from anxiety's grip and depression's clutches. Through the techniques explored in this chapter, you can embark on a transformative journey of self-care and discover the healing power of hydrotherapy in calming anxiety and uplifting Depression while promoting overall well-being. So, let's dive into the world of **hydrotherapy** and explore the many ways in which water can support us on our path to anxiety and depression relief.

Natural Hot Springs for the Mind

AS THE SUN RISES, casting its warm glow across the lush landscape, you find yourself standing at the edge of a hidden oasis nestled within a tranquil forest. The air is crisp and fragrant, carrying the sweet scent of pine and wildflowers. Invigorated by the beauty of your surroundings, you take a deep breath, inhaling the purity of nature into your lungs.

Following a narrow trail that winds its way through towering trees and delicate ferns, you can hear the gentle sounds of a babbling brook growing louder with each step. The anticipation builds within you, a sense of anticipation and excitement mixed with a calm reverence for what lies ahead.

As you emerge from the underbrush, a soft gasp escapes your lips as you behold the remarkable sight before you. A picture-perfect scene unfolds, revealing a series of natural hot springs, their crystal-clear waters cascading from one pool to the next in a mesmerizing display. Steam rises lazily from the surface, creating an ethereal mist that dances in rhythm with the sunlight filtering through the canopy above.

Making your way towards the closest pool, you dip your toes in, immediately feeling the warmth embrace your feet. The water sends ripples through your body, easing tension with every touch. The sensation is akin to being enveloped in a silky blanket of tranquility, a gentle hug from the earth itself.

Entering the water, you can feel its soothing caress embracing your body. The heat seeps deep into your muscles, releasing any knots and tightness that have built up from the weight of responsibilities. As you settle into the pool, your entire being sings with gratitude for this moment of respite.

Around you, the natural surroundings provide a breathtaking backdrop. Towering evergreen trees sway gently in the breeze, their branches whispering tales of ancient wisdom. Sunlight filters through the dense foliage, casting dappled patterns of light onto the water's surface, creating a mesmerizing array of colors. The vibrant hues of wildflowers that dot the landscape add a touch of delicate beauty to the scene, their petals reaching toward the heavens.

As you close your eyes, the sounds of nature serenade your senses. The gentle rustling of leaves, birdsong, and the distant melody of the flowing brook blend harmoniously, creating a symphony of peace and serenity. Each sound is a gentle reminder that you are part of something much more significant, a connected and intricate part of life.

With each passing minute, your body and mind surrender to the healing power of the hot springs. The weight of the world effortlessly melts away, replaced by a renewed sense of calm and inner peace. Your anxieties dissolve, replaced by a deep understanding of grounding and tranquility.

You take a moment to connect with the earth, feeling the coolness of the surrounding rocks against your fingertips. You let yourself be embraced by the energy of the earth, grounding yourself in its unwavering support. Here, at this moment, you are safe, held, and nurtured by the beauty of nature.

As time passes, the sun begins its descent, casting a golden glow upon the landscape. You reluctantly emerge from the warm embrace of the hot springs, feeling rejuvenated and reborn. You carry with you the serenity of this place, etching it into your memory as a sanctuary of peace.

With a thankful heart and renewed spirit, you make your way back along the trail, knowing that this hidden treasure will always be waiting in times of need, a sanctuary of relaxation and rejuvenation for your soul.

CHAPTER TWELVE

THE RESTORATIVE POWER OF SLEEP

ALLEVIATING ANXIETY AND DEPRESSION THROUGH QUALITY REST

Sleep is the best meditation. -Dalai Lama

IN THIS CHAPTER, WE will learn why sleep plays such a vital role in alleviating anxiety and reducing depression. Countless studies have shown that sleep profoundly impacts our mental and emotional well-being. While anxiety can disrupt **sleep** patterns, in turn, poor sleep can exacerbate depression symptoms. Understanding the intricate relationship between sleep and stress is crucial for developing effective strategies to manage anxiety and improve overall well-being. By prioritizing quality rest and implementing healthy **sleep** habits, we can tap into the transformative power of **sleep** to find relief from anxiety and depression.

The Sleep-Anxiety Connection:

Anxiety and sleep have a complex relationship. On the one hand, stress can lead to difficulty falling asleep, staying asleep, or experiencing restful sleep. Worries, racing thoughts, and physical tension often plague individuals with depression, making it challenging to relax and drift into a deep slumber. On the other hand, lack of sleep or poor sleep quality can contribute to increased anxiety levels, exacerbating worry and tension. This bidirectional link emphasizes the significance of prioritizing sleep for stress management.

The Benefits of Sleep for Anxiety and Depression:

Quality sleep offers a multitude of benefits to alleviate anxiety and promote overall well-being, including:

1. Reduction of Anxiety Symptoms: Adequate sleep allows the brain and body to rest and recover, aiding in regulating stress hormones such as cortisol. This can lead to a decrease in anxiety symptoms, such as excessive worry, irritability, and restlessness.

2. Emotional Regulation: Sleep plays a vital role in emotional regulation and resilience. Sufficient rest enhances the brain's ability to process and regulate emotions, helping individuals cope more effectively with stressors and depression triggers.

3. Cognitive Clarity: Sleep is essential for optimal cognitive function. A well-rested mind is better equipped to problem-solve, think creatively, and make rational decisions, reducing anxiety-inducing cognitive distortions and rumination.

4. Physical Restoration: Sleep provides an opportunity for the body to repair and rejuvenate. It helps to heal and restore tissues, regulate hormonal balance, and strengthen the immune system, ultimately reducing physical symptoms of depression, such as muscle tension and fatigue.

5. Mood Enhancement: A good night's sleep can significantly improve mood and emotional well-being. It increases the production of neurotransmitters like serotonin, a mood-regulating chemical that promotes feelings of happiness and relaxation, reducing depression symptoms.

Healthy Sleep Habits for Anxiety and Depression Relief:

Incorporating healthy sleep habits into your daily routine can significantly contribute to insomnia relief. Here are some strategies to enhance the quality of your sleep:

1. Establish a consistent sleep schedule: Go to bed and wake up at the same time each day to regulate your body's internal clock and promote a consistent sleep pattern.

2. Create a soothing bedtime routine: Engage in relaxing activities before bed, such as reading, taking a warm bath, practicing gentle stretches, or listening to calming music. These rituals signal to your mind and body that it is time to unwind and prepare for sleep.

3. Optimize your sleep environment: Create a sleep-friendly environment by keeping your bedroom cool, dark, and quiet. Invest in comfortable mattresses, pillows, and bedding to ensure physical comfort and support.

4. Limit exposure to electronic devices: The blue light emitted by electronic devices can disrupt the production of melatonin, a hormone essential for sleep. Avoid screens for at least an hour before bed to promote better sleep quality.

5. Practice relaxation techniques: Explore relaxation techniques such as deep breathing, progressive muscle relaxation, and meditation before bed to calm the mind and reduce anxiety before sleep.

Sleep is a fundamental pillar of our well-being, with significant implications for stress management. By understanding the intricate relationship between sleep and anxiety, we can prioritize quality rest as a powerful tool in alleviating depression symptoms. The benefits of sleep for anxiety relief are multi-faceted, improving emotional regulation, cognitive clarity, physical restoration, and overall mood. By implementing healthy sleep habits and cultivating a restorative sleep routine, we can harness the transformative power of sleep and pave the way for greater calm, balance, and well-being in our lives. So, prepare to embrace the refreshing embrace of sleep as we explore the profound impact it can have on alleviating anxiety and depression.

1. I easily fall into a deep and restful sleep every night.

2. My body and mind naturally unwind and relax as I prepare for sleep.

3. I release all tension and stress before bed, allowing my body to rejuvenate fully.

4. Each morning, I wake up feeling refreshed and energized.

5. My bedroom is a sanctuary of peace and tranquility, promoting restful sleep.

6. I deserve the gift of a good night's sleep and allow myself to embrace it fully.

7. My sleep is consistent and uninterrupted, providing me with the rest I need.

8. I welcome peaceful dreams and wake up feeling inspired and motivated.

9. I am grateful for the healing power of sleep and the restoration it brings to my body and mind.

10. My mind and body naturally align with the rhythm of natural sleep cycles.

Serenity Dream Sleep

IMAGINE YOURSELF IN A peaceful meadow nestled among rolling green hills. The sun is setting, casting a warm, golden glow over the landscape. As you lay down on the soft grass, you can feel the gentle breeze caressing your skin, soothing away any tension or worry.

As you take a deep breath, you notice the scent of wildflowers that fill the air. Their delicate fragrance, a sweet symphony, calms your mind and invites relaxation. The chirping of birds, hidden among the branches of the nearby trees, creates a soothing melody, weaving a symphony of tranquility around you.

You close your eyes and visualize a stream flowing nearby. Picture the mesmerizing dance of water as it gracefully winds its way through the meadow, glistening in the fading sunlight. Each ripple and babbling sound brings with it a sense of serenity and tranquility, washing away any lingering stress or anxiety.

As your gaze shifts upwards, you see the sky transform into a vivid canvas of hues. Shades of pink, orange, and purple blend together, slowly dissolving into a soft, velvety blue. The first stars begin to appear, twinkling in the vastness of the night sky. Your eyes feel heavy in the dimming light.

You continue your journey into relaxation by envisioning a blanket of fluffy, soft clouds floating above. Watch as they shape-shift into delightful figures, like animals and familiar objects, as the night envelopes you, making your eyes grow even heavier. You let your imagination wander and play, allowing your mind to let go of any worries or concerns that may have resurfaced during the day. Taking in a big yawn and releasing into the exhale, you feel the warm relaxation of the night covering you like a cozy blanket.

Now, imagine yourself being gently cradled by the earth beneath you. Feel the supportive energy of the ground beneath your body, grounding you and providing a sense of security. Imagine roots extending from your body, sinking deep into the earth, absorbing its nourishing energy.

With each exhale, release any tension you may be holding onto, allowing it to dissipate into the earth. As you inhale, feel a renewed sense of calm and tranquility wash over you like a gentle wave. Imagine this wave of relaxation spreading from the top of your head, flowing down through your body, releasing any remaining tension or anxiety.

As you drift deeper into relaxation, imagine a soft, warm purple light enveloping you, cocooning you in a soothing embrace. This light is filled with peace, love, and healing energy, gently lulling you to sleep. Feel its comforting presence, wrapping around you like a cozy comforter, ensuring a restful and revitalizing slumber. Allow a gentle yawn of gratitude.

As you surrender to the sensations of peace and relaxation, allow yourself to let go and fall into a deep, peaceful sleep. Trust in the power of these visualizations to guide you towards restful dreams, knowing that you are safe, supported, and deserving of a night filled with calmness.

Let this visualization be your sanctuary, your peaceful haven where you can always return to find refuge from the storms of anxiety. As you drift off to sleep, may you find solace and wake up feeling refreshed and ready to embrace a new day filled with peace and joy.

CHAPTER THIRTEEN

AFFIRMATIONS TRANSFORM NEGATIVE THINKING

THE SEEDS OF AFFIRMATIONS FOR OVERCOMING ANXIETY AND DEPRESSION

Affirmations are like seeds planted in the garden of your mind with nurturing and belief, they grow into the reality you desire. -Louise Hay

AFFIRMATIONS ARE POSITIVE STATEMENTS that are repeated regularly to help retrain the subconscious mind and shift negative thought patterns. When it comes to anxiety, affirmations can be a powerful tool for calming the mind, reducing stress, and building resilience.

Depression often stems from negative and fear-based thoughts that loop in our minds, creating a cycle of worry and unease. Affirmations work by replacing these negative thoughts with positive and empowering statements. They help to reprogram the mind and instill a new belief system that counteracts depressive thoughts.

Regularly Repeating Affirmations: We Can!

1. Shift our mindset: Affirmations help us to consciously choose positive thoughts and beliefs, even in the face of depression. They can counteract the self-doubt and negative thinking patterns that often accompany depression.

2. Build self-confidence: Anxiety often erodes our self-esteem and belief in our abilities. Affirmations can build our self-confidence by reminding us of our strengths, resilience, and the positive qualities we possess.

3. Cultivate a sense of calm: Affirmations can create a state of calm and relaxation by redirecting our focus away from anxious thoughts. They can help to soothe the mind and lower stress levels, allowing us to approach situations with greater ease and clarity.

4. Foster a positive outlook: Ongoing depression can cloud our perspective and lead us to expect the worst in every situation. Affirmations can help us develop and maintain a positive outlook, allowing us to approach challenges with optimism and hope.

Positive Affirmations for Overcoming Anxiety and Depression:

Here are some positive affirmations that can be helpful in overcoming anxiety and depression. Please use these affirmations in any creative fashion you might benefit from. Put them on your ceiling to wake up to, and try saying them out loud for the most benefit. Write them on cue cards and place them everywhere they might surprise you: in your purse or desk, in a friend's pocket. **They are here to remind us who we are.** Share them and shout them out loud, or do whatever feels right and have fun! The last #101 is for your personal affirmation to you. Remember, the key to getting the most out of affirmations is to repeat them regularly and believe in their power to create positive change in your life. With practice and persistence, affirmations can become a valuable tool in overcoming everyday challenges and living a more peaceful and fulfilling life.

101 Powerful Affirmations for Anxiety and Depression

Notice Whatever Arises While Repeating Aloud

1. I am calm, centered, and at peace.

2. I release all worries and embrace the present moment.

3. I trust in my ability to handle any challenges that come my way.

4. I am stronger than my depression, and I can overcome it.

5. I replace fear with love and compassion.

6. My mind is clear, focused, and free from anxiety.

7. I BREATHE IN RELAXATION AND EXHALE TENSION.

8. I AM IN CONTROL OF MY THOUGHTS AND EMOTIONS.

9. I CHOOSE PEACE AND HAPPINESS OVER DEPRESSION.

10. I AM WORTHY OF A LIFE FREE FROM ANXIETY.

11. I RELEASE ALL NEGATIVE THOUGHTS AND EMBRACE POSITIVITY.

12. I ATTRACT CALMNESS AND TRANQUILITY INTO MY LIFE.

13. I AM SAFE AND PROTECTED AT EVERY MOMENT.

14. I HAVE THE POWER TO OVERCOME MY ANXIETY AND LIVE A FULFILLING LIFE.

15. I AM RESILIENT AND CAN BOUNCE BACK FROM ANY SETBACKS.

16. I AM SURROUNDED BY LOVING AND SUPPORTIVE PEOPLE WHO UPLIFT ME.

17. I RELEASE THE NEED TO COMPARE MYSELF TO OTHERS AND EMBRACE MY UNIQUENESS.

18. I AM CAPABLE OF HANDLING ANYTHING THAT COMES MY WAY.

19. I CHOOSE TO FOCUS ON THE PRESENT MOMENT RATHER THAN WORRYING ABOUT THE FUTURE.

20. I AM IN CONTROL OF MY BREATHING, AND I CAN CALM MY MIND AND BODY.

21. I RELEASE ALL EXPECTATIONS AND ALLOW LIFE TO UNFOLD NATURALLY.

22. I DESERVE TO LIVE WITH PEACE AND JOY.

23. I LET GO OF PAST REGRETS AND POSITIVELY EMBRACE MY FUTURE.

24. I AM GRATEFUL FOR WHAT I HAVE AND EXCITED FOR WHAT IS TO COME.

25. I RELEASE THE NEED FOR PERFECTION AND EMBRACE MY IMPERFECTIONS.

26. I TRUST IN THE WISDOM OF MY BODY AND MIND TO GUIDE ME THROUGH ANXIETY.

27. I AM DESERVING OF LOVE AND SUPPORT, ESPECIALLY DURING MOMENTS OF DEPRESSION.

28. MY DEPRESSION DOES NOT DEFINE ME; MY STRENGTH AND RESILIENCE DEFINE ME.

29. I CHOOSE TO SEE CHALLENGES AS OPPORTUNITIES FOR GROWTH AND LEARNING.

30. I RELEASE ALL WORRIES AND SURRENDER TO THE FLOW OF LIFE.

31. I HAVE THE POWER TO CHANGE MY THOUGHTS AND REWRITE MY STORY.

32. I TRUST IN THE PROCESS OF LIFE AND KNOW THAT EVERYTHING WILL WORK OUT FOR MY HIGHEST GOOD.

33. My mind is a sanctuary of peace and tranquility.

34. I am surrounded by the positive energy that uplifts and supports me.

35. I can find solutions and create a life filled with peace and serenity.

36. I choose to focus on the things I can control and let go of the rest.

37. I am deserving of peace, happiness, and an anxiety-free life.

38. I am open to receiving love and support from myself and others.

39. I forgive myself for past mistakes and release any guilt or shame.

40. I am grounded and connected to the present moment.

41. I trust in my intuition to guide me toward the right path.

42. I am resilient and capable of adapting to change.

43. I embrace uncertainty with curiosity and excitement.

44. I have the strength to face my fears and overcome them.

45. I AM GRATEFUL FOR THE LESSONS THAT ANXIETY HAS TAUGHT ME.

46. I RELEASE ALL NEGATIVE ENERGY AND WELCOME POSITIVITY INTO MY LIFE.

47. I AM IN TUNE WITH MY BODY'S NEEDS AND CARE FOR MYSELF WITH LOVE AND COMPASSION.

48. I AM CAPABLE OF FINDING PEACE AND SERENITY WITHIN MYSELF.

49. I AM NOT ALONE; THERE ARE PEOPLE WHO LOVE AND SUPPORT ME.

50. MY DEPRESSION DOES NOT DEFINE ME; I AM DEFINED BY MY COURAGE TO FACE IT.

51. I RELEASE ALL EXPECTATIONS AND EMBRACE THE PRESENT MOMENT AS IT IS.

52. I AM WORTHY OF ALL THE GOOD THINGS THAT LIFE HAS TO OFFER.

53. I TRUST IN THE PROCESS OF HEALING AND KNOW THAT I AM ON THE RIGHT PATH.

54. I CAN CREATE A LIFE FILLED WITH JOY AND PEACE.

55. I RELEASE ALL FEARS AND ALLOW LOVE TO GUIDE ME.

56. I AM ENOUGH JUST AS I AM AND DON'T NEED TO PROVE MYSELF TO ANYONE.

57. I AM STRONGER THAN I THINK AND CAN OVERCOME ANY CHALLENGE.

58. I LET GO OF THE NEED TO CONTROL EVERYTHING AND TRUST THE UNIVERSE'S GUIDANCE.

59. I AM WORTHY OF SELF-CARE AND TAKING TIME TO NOURISH MY WELL-BEING.

60. I AM DESERVING OF LOVE, ACCEPTANCE, AND UNDERSTANDING.

61. I LET GO OF THE PAST AND EMBRACE THE PRESENT MOMENT WITH GRATITUDE.

62. MY ANXIETY DOES NOT DEFINE ME; MY RESILIENCE AND INNER STRENGTH DEFINE ME.

63. I CHOOSE TO FOCUS ON THE POSITIVES IN MY LIFE AND LET GO OF NEGATIVITY.

64. I RELEASE ALL WORRIES ABOUT THE FUTURE AND TRUST EVERYTHING WILL WORK OUT.

65. INFINITE POSSIBILITIES AND OPPORTUNITIES SURROUND ME.

66. I AM WORTHY OF HAPPINESS, PEACE, AND FULFILLMENT.

67. I AM SAFE AND PROTECTED AT ALL TIMES.

68. I RELEASE THE NEED TO PLEASE OTHERS AND FOCUS ON MY OWN WELL-BEING.

69. I AM IN CONTROL OF MY THOUGHTS, EMOTIONS, AND REACTIONS.

70. I TRUST IN THE JOURNEY OF SELF-DISCOVERY AND KNOW THAT EVERY STEP FORWARD IS PROGRESS.

71. I AM GRATEFUL FOR MY BODY AND TREAT IT WITH LOVE AND RESPECT.

72. I RELEASE ALL CONSTRAINTS AND FREELY EXPRESS WHO I AM.

73. I AM LOVED AND VALUED BY THOSE AROUND ME.

74. I AM OPEN TO RECEIVING SUPPORT AND GUIDANCE FROM THE UNIVERSE.

75. I CHOOSE TO SEE CHALLENGES AS OPPORTUNITIES FOR GROWTH AND TRANSFORMATION.

76. I AM DESERVING OF A LIFE FILLED WITH EASE AND GRACE.

77. I TRUST IN MY ABILITY TO HANDLE ANY SITUATION THAT ARISES.

78. I AM NOT ALONE IN MY STRUGGLE; THERE ARE OTHERS WHO UNDERSTAND AND SUPPORT ME.

79. I RELEASE ALL THOUGHTS THAT NO LONGER SERVE ME AND REPLACE THEM WITH EMPOWERING BELIEFS.

80. I AM CAPABLE OF BRINGING MY DREAMS AND ASPIRATIONS TO LIFE.

81. I RELEASE ALL FEARS OF JUDGMENT AND EMBRACE MY AUTHENTIC SELF.

82. I TRUST IN THE POWER OF MY MIND TO OVERCOME ANXIETY AND CREATE A LIFE OF PEACE.

83. I AM FLEXIBLE AND ADAPTABLE, ABLE TO NAVIGATE THROUGH ANY CHALLENGES THAT COME MY WAY.

84. I AM GROUNDED AND ROOTED IN MY STRENGTH AND RESILIENCE.

85. I CHOOSE TO BE KIND TO MYSELF AND PRACTICE SELF-COMPASSION.

86. I AM DESERVING OF REST, RELAXATION, AND REJUVENATION.

87. I TRUST IN THE HEALING PROCESS AND KNOW I AM PROGRESSING.

88. I RELEASE ALL EXPECTATIONS AND SURRENDER TO THE FLOW OF LIFE.

89. I CAN CREATE A LIFE FILLED WITH JOY, LOVE, AND ABUNDANCE.

90. I AM GRATEFUL FOR THE LESSONS THAT DEPRESSION HAS TAUGHT ME AND THE GROWTH IT HAS FACILITATED.

91. I RELEASE ALL WORRIES AND TRUST IN THE DIVINE PLAN FOR MY LIFE.

92. I DESERVE ALL THE GOOD THINGS THAT COME MY WAY.

93. I AM SURROUNDED BY LOVE, PEACE, AND SUPPORT.

94. I CHOOSE TO LET GO OF FEAR AND EMBRACE LOVE IN EVERY ASPECT OF MY LIFE.

95. I HAVE THE STRENGTH AND RESILIENCE TO OVERCOME ANY CHALLENGES THAT COME MY WAY.

96. I CONTROL MY THOUGHTS AND CHOOSE TO FOCUS ON POSITIVITY.

97. I DESERVE HAPPINESS AND FULFILLMENT IN ALL AREAS OF MY LIFE.

98. I TRUST IN LIFE AND KNOW THAT EVERYTHING HAPPENS FOR A REASON.

99. I RELEASE ALL WORRIES ABOUT THE FUTURE AND TRUST THAT THE UNIVERSE HAS A PLAN FOR ME.

100. I AM A BEACON OF LIGHT, RADIATING PEACE AND TRANQUILITY TO THOSE AROUND ME.

101. (WRITE YOUR OWN SPECIAL ONE!)

Use these **affirmations as often as you can,** practice them aloud, and notice any emotions or feelings that may arise as you repeat them. Try to "**march**" your way through all **101** and see which ones resonate with you the most.

Affirmations will solidify all of your work toward holistic health.

Chapter Fourteen

Visualizations Unleash Creativity

The Power of Visualizations in Overcoming Anxiety and Depression

Visualization is daydreaming with a purpose. -Bo Bennett

WELCOME TO THIS CHAPTER on the transformative power of visualizations. In this chapter, we will explore how visualizations can be an effective tool in helping individuals cope with and overcome anxiety and depression. These two ailments are shared experiences that affect millions of people worldwide, often resulting in feelings of restlessness, worry, and fear. While both can be overwhelming and challenging to manage, the good news is that there are various techniques available to support individuals in their journey toward healing and inner peace. One such technique is the power of visualizations.

Before diving into the heart of visualizations, it is essential to understand the nature of stress-induced mental turmoil. Anxiety is not simply a product of our external circumstances but is deeply rooted in our thoughts, emotions, and beliefs. It can be triggered by a wide range of factors, such as past experiences, expectations, and societal pressures. Unchecked, anxiety can negatively impact our mental, emotional, and even physical well-being. Therefore, it is crucial to address anxiety holistically, taking into account the interconnectedness of mind-body and spirit. By also addressing our subconscious mind through visualizations we can achieve holistic health.

Similarly to anxiety, depression is not solely caused by external circumstances but is influenced by a complex interplay between biological, psychological, and social factors. Depression is characterized by persistent feelings of sadness, hopelessness, and a loss of interest in activities that were once enjoyed. It affects how we think, feel, and behave and can lead to a significant decrease in quality of life.

Biologically, depression is associated with imbalances in certain neurotransmitters, such as **serotonin, norepinephrine, and dopamine**. These chemicals play crucial roles in regulating mood, emotions, and motivation. Additionally, genetic factors can predispose individuals to develop depression.

Psychologically, negative thought patterns, such as rumination, self-criticism, and a negative view of oneself, others, and the world, can contribute to the onset and maintenance of depression. Traumatic experiences, unresolved conflicts, and low self-esteem can also be significant factors.

Socially, factors such as a lack of social support, relationship problems, financial difficulties, and isolation can contribute to the development of depression. Additionally, societal pressures and cultural expectations can play a role in exacerbating depressive symptoms.

Treating depression requires a holistic approach that addresses all these interconnected factors. Along with seeking professional help, various strategies can be beneficial in managing depression.

One proven beneficial strategy that has therapeutic results for both anxiety and depression is in the power of visualizations.

What are Visualizations?

Visualizations are powerful mental imagery exercises that allow individuals to create vivid and sensory-rich experiences in their minds. By engaging in guided visualizations, individuals can activate their imagination and tap into the infinite potential of their minds. Visualizations involve creating mental pictures, sounds, and sensations that evoke positive emotions and a sense of calm. They enable individuals to connect with their inner resources, resilience, and wisdom, enabling them to navigate their journey to holistic health with greater ease and clarity.

Visualizations have been used for centuries across various cultures and traditions as a tool for healing, manifestation, and personal growth. They are based on the understanding that the mind-body connection is incredibly powerful and that the thoughts and images we hold in our minds can influence our physical, mental, and emotional well-being.

When practicing visualizations, individuals actively engage their senses to create a multisensory experience in their minds. For example, if someone is visualizing themselves in a peaceful forest, they may imagine the vibrant colors of the trees, feel the soft grass beneath their feet, hear the sound of birds chirping, and even smell the scent of the flowers. By engaging all the senses, the experience becomes more vivid and immersive, enhancing the effectiveness of the visualization.

The benefits of visualizations extend beyond the imagination. Research has shown that when individuals engage in vivid visualizations, their brain activity changes, and **neural pathways associated with positive emotions, creativity, and problem-solving are activated**. As a result, visualizations can have a profound impact on reducing stress, improving sleep, boosting self-confidence, managing pain, and even enhancing performance in various areas of life, such as sports and public speaking.

To effectively practice visualizations, it is essential to create a calm and quiet environment where you can fully immerse yourself in the experience. You can find guided visualizations online or create your own by focusing on a specific goal or desired outcome. Whether you visualize yourself achieving your dreams, overcoming a challenge, or simply relaxing and rejuvenating, the key is to hold the intention and belief that you are creating a positive shift within yourself.

Incorporating visualizations into your daily routine can have a transformative effect on your overall well-being. Just a few minutes of visualization each day can help you tap into your inner wisdom, cultivate a positive mindset, and create the life you desire. So, take a moment to close your eyes, engage your senses, and embark on a journey of self-discovery and transformation through the power of visualizations.

How Visualizations Help with Anxiety and Depression:

Visualizations offer a unique approach to managing stress by directing our focus towards more positive and empowering states of mind. When we engage in visualizations, we are essentially **rewiring our brains and reprogramming our thought patterns**. Visualizing ourselves in calming and reassuring scenarios can create a sense of safety and serenity within ourselves. Visualizations also allow us to shift our perspective and challenge the negative and distorted thinking that often accompanies anxiety and depression. Through consistent practice, visualizations can enhance our self-awareness and enable us to develop healthy coping mechanisms for managing and reducing negative emotions.

Benefits of Visualizations for Anxiety and Depression:

The benefits of incorporating visualizations into a stress-management practice are manifold. By regularly engaging in visualizations, individuals can experience the following:

1. Reduced stress levels: Visualizations induce a relaxation response in the body, leading to decreased physiological and psychological tension.

2. Enhanced self-soothing abilities: Visualizations provide individuals with the tools to calm themselves and soothe their anxieties during moments of stress or panic.

3. Greater clarity and focus: Visualizations help individuals redirect their attention away from anxious thoughts and onto positive mental images, which can enhance concentration and mental clarity.

4. Increased self-confidence: Visualizations can elevate self-confidence by fostering a deeper connection with one's inner strengths and resources.

5. Improved overall well-being: Regular practice of visualizations can contribute to overall well-being by promoting feelings of peace, joy, and resilience.

Visualizations offer a powerful and accessible tool for those seeking relief from brutal emotional and mental anguish. Through the practice of mental imagery and intentional focus, individuals can tap into their innate ability to foster a sense of calm, inner strength, and resilience. In the following chapters of this book, we will explore various visualization techniques and exercises tailored specifically to address different aspects of emotional turmoil, empowering you in your journey toward healing and lasting transformation. Remember, you have the power to overcome anxiety and depression. Visualizations are an invaluable tool on this path to emotional well-being and personal growth.

Visualizations for Peace and Serenity

Tranquil Beach Retreat

C LOSE YOUR EYES AND find yourself transported to a tropical paradise. You stand on a pristine, sandy beach. The grains are cool and comforting beneath your bare feet. Surrounding you is a dazzling expanse of clear, turquoise water that stretches as far as the eye can see. The gentle lapping of waves against the shore serenades your ears, creating a soothing melody of tranquility.

The sun radiates its warmth upon your skin, creating a delightful caress that relaxes every muscle in your body. A gentle breeze dances upon your face, carrying with it the scent of salt and the faint fragrance of tropical flora. The air is alive with vibrant, tropical birds singing melodic tunes, adding to the enchanting ambiance.

As you walk along the beach, you feel the softness of the sand beneath your toes, each step sinking slightly, leaving behind an imprint that is quickly erased by the receding tide. The cool water rushes over your feet with a gentle touch, refreshing and invigorating. You continue your leisurely stroll, taking in the breathtaking view of the endless horizon where the sky seamlessly merges with the sea in shades of blue and gold.

Finding the perfect spot on the beach, you settle down on a plush beach towel. Gazing up at the clear blue sky, you feel a sense of complete ease wash over you. Any worries or tensions that may have weighed on your mind dissolve with every passing wave. The rhythmic crashes of the ocean's embrace with the shore become a soothing lullaby, lulling you into deep relaxation.

In this moment of serenity, you can feel the vibrant energy of the beach enveloping you. The salty air fills your lungs, each breath bringing a sense of purity and rejuvenation. You become acutely aware of your body, the rise and fall of each inhale and exhale, with the peaceful rhythm of the waves.

Imagine a sudden urge to immerse yourself in the crystal-clear water that beckons you. As you dive into the sea, you experience a remarkable sensation of weightlessness. The coolness of the water envelops your body, washing away any remaining stress or anxiety that may cling to your soul. It is as if the ocean's embrace holds the power to cleanse and restore.

As you swim, picture gentle sea creatures gracefully gliding by, moving with a serene sense of peace and tranquility. Colorful tropical fish dart playfully through the coral reefs, their vibrant hues akin to a living rainbow. Gently touch the delicate sea plants, feeling the texture of the underwater world beneath your fingertips. Allow the sense of calmness and relaxation to wash over you, filling every cell of your being.

Stay in this peaceful visualization for as long as you desire, allowing the serene atmosphere of the beach to permeate your mind, body, and soul. Let the magical nature of this tropical paradise envelop you, providing a haven of tranquility and rejuvenation. When you are ready to return to the present moment, take a deep breath and slowly open your eyes, bringing the sense of contentment and tranquility you have cultivated.

Serene Mountain Retreat

PLEASE CLOSE YOUR EYES and imagine yourself standing at the base of a majestic mountain range, its peaks reaching upward toward the heavens. The sky is a brilliant blue, adorned with fluffy white clouds that cast shadows on the terrain below. The air is pure and invigorating, wafting the scent of pine and the promise of adventure.

As you begin your ascent, you find yourself on a winding path that cuts through a dense forest. The towering trees stretch towards the sky, their branches intertwined in a delicate dance. Shafts of sunlight filter through the gaps in the canopy, casting ethereal beams illuminating the path ahead. The forest floor is carpeted with moss, a plush cushion beneath your feet as if nature is guiding your steps.

As you climb, the forest comes alive with a symphony of sound. The melodious chirping of birds fills the air, their colorful plumage a vibrant contrast against the lush green foliage. The gentle rustling of leaves creates a soothing backdrop, as if nature is whispering secrets only known to the wind. A nearby stream gurgles playfully, its crystal-clear waters cascading over rocks, creating a gentle song.

The temperature gradually drops with each step, and the air becomes crisper. The scent of pine grows stronger, reminding you of the ancient wisdom residing within these mountains. You feel a sense of lightness and freedom as the world below fades from view. It's as if the mountain's embrace lifts you higher, carrying you closer to the heavens.

After a steady climb, you reach a breathtaking viewpoint, perched on a rocky outcrop that overlooks a panorama of awe-inspiring beauty. The emerald valleys unfold before you, embracing rolling hills and meadows that stretch as far as the eye can see. The meadows are adorned with a pastel checkerboard of wildflowers, their vibrant petals reaching toward the heavens in a joyful display of nature's artistry. The sunbeams dance upon the landscape, casting a soft golden glow upon the scene.

Finding a comfortable sitting spot, you rest upon the cool stone, feeling its rough texture against your fingertips. As you close your eyes, you surrender to the serenity and beauty surrounding you. The sounds of nature fill your ears - the soft hum of bees as they gather nectar, the gentle rustle of leaves as they sway in the breeze, the distant trickle of a waterfall cascading down the mountainside. It's as if nature is conducting a masterpiece, and you are fortunate enough to be part of the audience.

You place your hands on the ground, feeling its warmth beneath your palms. Imagining roots extending from your fingertips, you visualize them sinking deep into the earth, anchoring you to the mountain's solid foundation. The mountains become your ally, lending you strength and stability. A profound sense of peace and grounding washes over you as if you are one with the mountain.

As you sit in this serene retreat, you let your gaze wander over the vast expanse before you. The colors of the landscape come alive, each hue more vibrant than the last—shades of green dance through the trees, infused with a golden radiance from the sunlight. The wildflowers paint a breathtaking sound of blues, purples, pinks, and yellows, blending together in a cascade of color. The mountain peaks, stoic and majestic, rise like sentinels, their peaks dusted with a delicate layer of snow that glints in the sunlight.

As you take in the splendor of the mountain retreat, you can't help but feel a sense of gratitude for being able to experience this moment of pure tranquility. The worries and stresses of the outside world seem distant and less significant in this serene setting.

Take a deep breath, allowing the pure mountain air to fill your lungs. With each exhale, you release any lingering tension or worries, surrendering them to the open space around you. As you do so, you feel a profound sense of calmness settles within, like a still lake reflecting the majesty of the mountains.

You may choose to stay here for a while longer, breathing in the fresh mountain air and allowing the soothing sounds of nature to envelop you. As you sit in stillness, you feel a deep connection to the earth and all living beings. You realize that just as the mountain stands strong and unwavering, you can also find your own resilience and inner strength.

What qualities do you want to cultivate in yourself? Whether it is peace, patience, or courage, envision these qualities spreading throughout your being, emanating from the core of your being like ripples on a calm mountain lake.

Take a moment to set an intention for the days ahead. When you feel ready to return to the present moment, stand up slowly, feeling the solid ground beneath your feet.

As you begin your descent down the mountain, take a moment to express gratitude for the experience and the insights gained. Carry this sense of peace and connection with you as you integrate it into your daily life.

As you make your way down the mountain, you find that each step becomes a gentle reminder to stay present and grounded. The air around you feels lighter, and the sunlight filters through the tree canopy, creating playful patterns of light and shadow along the trail.

With each breath, you release any lingering tensions, allowing the mountain's tranquility to infuse your entire being. The sounds of chirping birds and rustling leaves remind you of nature, guiding you deeper into a state of peace and contentment.

As you continue your descent, you come across a small clearing bathed in warm sunlight. You decide to take a moment to sit and reflect on your journey. Closing your eyes, you listen to the soft murmurs of the wind and feel the gentle caress of the sunlight on your skin. In this stillness, you allow your mind to quiet, noticing any thoughts or emotions that arise and letting them pass like clouds crossing the sky.

You recognize that this mountain retreat has become a sanctuary of clarity and insight, where you can realign with your deepest self and find solace in the gentle rhythms of nature. From this place of centeredness, you gain a renewed sense of purpose and direction, knowing that you can carry the tranquility and wisdom of the mountains with you wherever you go.

With a sense of gratitude, you open your eyes and stand up, feeling a newfound lightness in your step. As you resume your descent, you take one last look up at the majestic mountain, the source of your inspiration and newfound peace.

With a heart full of gratitude for this unique experience, you continue on your journey, carrying the serenity and wisdom of this mountain retreat within you. Remember that whenever life's challenges arise, you can always return to this inner sanctuary to reconnect with your inner strength and find solace in the beauty of the natural world. This is a sacred space within your mind and heart, a sanctuary of calm amidst the busyness of life.

Lush Forest Oasis

CLOSE YOUR EYES AND transport yourself to a dense, vibrant, green forest. As you step into this enchanting realm, the sounds of nature greet you with a symphony of life. Birds chirp and sing melodious tunes, their voices weaving through the trees and filling the air with joyous melodies. The leaves rustle in a gentle breeze, creating a soothing whisper that dances with the forest song. In the distance, a nearby stream babbles and gurgles, its gentle flow a constant reminder of the life-giving force of water.

As you stroll through the forest, you feel the softness of the moss and grass beneath your feet. Each step is a sensory delight, as the earth cushions your footsteps and connects you with the fertile ground. Rays of sunlight filter through the canopy above, casting dappled patterns of light and shadow on the forest floor. It's as if nature creates a playful dance just for you.

Breathe deeply, filling your lungs with the fresh, oxygen-rich air surrounding you. As you exhale, release any tension or anxiety weighing you down, surrendering it to the forest's embrace. Let the tranquility of this lush oasis wash over you, rejuvenating your spirit and setting your mind at ease.

As you continue your gentle walk, you stumble upon a clearing—a hidden haven within the forest's heart. The clearing is bathed in golden sunlight, creating an ethereal glow that illuminates the beauty of this sacred space. Picture a magnificent waterfall, its clear waters cascading down a rocky cliff, like nature's masterpiece in motion. The sound of water crashing fills the air, a tranquil cascade that resonates deep within your soul.

A gentle mist rises from the pool's surface at the waterfall's base, creating a relaxed and refreshing atmosphere. Find a comfortable spot near the pool and let the sound of the water wash away any remaining stress or worry. As you sit or lie down, be fully present in this serene sanctuary.

Imagine dipping your toes into the pool, feeling the coolness envelope your feet. The water caresses your skin, flowing between your toes and leaving a soothing trail in its wake. Slowly, immerse yourself in the water, feeling its gentle weightlessness as it supports your body. As your body becomes one with the water, feel your worries and anxieties dissolve and wash away, replaced by a profound sense of calm and serenity.

Allow yourself to float, surrendering to the gentle currents that guide you. Feel the water cradle you like a loving embrace from the forest itself. At this moment, time slows down, and you are entirely immersed in the healing energy of this sacred oasis. The water embraces you, washing away any lingering tension and filling you with a profound sense of peace.

Stay in this peaceful forest oasis for as long as you need, allowing the healing energy of nature to soothe your mind and body. Let the sounds of the waterfall and the caress of the water envelop you, rejuvenating your spirit and nourishing your soul. As you float and surrender to the magic of this serene sanctuary, feel your worries and cares melt away, leaving you with a renewed sense of peace and tranquility.

When you are ready to return to the present moment, take a deep breath, filling your lungs with pure forest air. As you exhale, release any lingering tension and slowly open your eyes. Carry with you the tranquility and serenity of this lush forest oasis, knowing that you can always revisit this sacred space in your mind and find comfort whenever you need it.

CHAPTER FIFTEEN

THE POWER OF SOCIAL CONNECTIONS

BUILDING BRIDGES TO JOY AND RESILIENCE

Health is a state of complete physical, mental and social well-being, not merely the absence of disease or infirm ity.-World Health Organization

ANXIETY, OFTEN CHARACTERIZED BY excessive worry and fear, can be a complex and challenging experience. While the journey to managing depression may seem daunting, one remarkable asset in this battle lies in the power of social connections. This chapter explores the pivotal role of social support and interpersonal relationships in anxiety treatment and depression management. From understanding the science behind social connections to exploring practical ways to enhance social interactions, we will embark on an uplifting and empowering journey toward creating a vibrant web of relationships that fosters healing and resilience.

Depression and anxiety can Both Impact Social Connections, but they do so in Different Ways:

Depression often leads to a withdrawal from social interactions. **Individuals with depression may isolate themselves,** avoid social activities, and **have difficulty initiating or maintaining relationships.** They may feel a lack of enjoyment or interest in socializing, have low self-esteem and negative self-perceptions, and struggle to connect with others emotionally. Depression can also affect communication and interpersonal skills, making it challenging to express oneself and engage with others effectively.

Humans Are Social Creatures Or Why Having Relationships Helps Relieve Anxiety and Depression:

As humans, we are inherently social creatures. From the moment we are born, we crave connection and interaction with others. Our brains are wired to seek out social bonds and navigate the complex web of social relationships. However, this natural inclination towards social connection can become a source of stress and apprehension for individuals with depression. In this chapter, we look into the fascinating world of the social brain, exploring the biological foundations that drive our social behavior and understanding how stress and anxiety can impact our ability to navigate the social landscape.

The Social Brain Hypothesis:

The social brain hypothesis proposes that the large size and complexity of the human brain evolved to support our intricate social lives. Unlike many other animals, humans live in complex social networks, requiring the ability to understand and react to the thoughts, emotions, and intentions of others.

Mirror Neurons:

Discovered in the 1990s, they play a crucial role in our ability to understand and empathize with others. These neurons fire when we perform an action and observe someone else performing the same activity. They allow us to mimic and understand the actions, emotions, and intentions of others, facilitating social learning and bonding.

Oxytocin:

Often referred to as the "love hormone," Oxytocin is a power-ful neurochemical involved in social bonding and trust. It is released during positive social interactions, physical touch, and acts of kindness. Oxytocin promotes feelings of empathy, cooperation, and connection, fostering healthy social relationships. Oxytocin is often called the "love hormone" because it plays a significant role in helping us build relationships with others and feel connected to them. It's a chemical that our brains release during positive social interactions. For example, when we hug someone we care about, our brains release Oxytocin. This hormone helps us feel closer to that person and creates a sense of trust and bonding. It also gets released when we engage in acts of kindness or have physical touch with others.

Oxytocin has many benefits for our relationships. It makes us feel more empathetic toward others so we can better understand and share their feelings. It also encourages cooperation, so we're more likely to work together and help each other.

Overall, Oxytocin helps create a warm and loving atmosphere in our social interactions. It strengthens our connections with others and promotes healthy relationships. Its effects are even more significant in close relationships, such as with partners, family, or close friends.

Social Anxiety: The Fear of Social Interaction:

Social Anxiety:

It is a common disorder characterized by an intense fear of social situations and of being judged, embarrassed, or humiliated by others. It can significantly impact an individual's ability to interact socially and lead to feelings of isolation and distress. Imagine you're at a party, surrounded by a group of people chatting and having a good time. But instead of feeling comfortable and joining in on the fun, you feel a surge of anxiety. Your heart starts racing, your palms get sweaty, and you can only think about how people might judge you. This, my friend, is what social anxiety feels like.

Social anxiety is an anxiety disorder where people experience an overwhelming fear of social situations. It's not just about being shy or nervous in unfamiliar situations. Social anxiety takes those feelings to a whole new level. It can make even the most straightforward social interactions, like going out to dinner with friends or speaking up in a meeting, appear as an insurmountable challenge.

People with social anxiety constantly fear being judged, embarrassed, or humiliated by others. They worry about saying or doing something "wrong" that will make them look foolish or stand out negatively. The thought of being the center of attention or having all eyes on them can trigger a cascade of anxiety symptoms. These can include a racing heart, sweaty palms, shortness of breath, trembling, or even a full-blown panic attack.

Because of these intense fears, individuals with social anxiety often avoid social situations as much as possible. They may decline invitations to parties, avoid speaking up in group conversations, or do everything they can to fly under the radar. While these avoidance behaviors may provide temporary relief, they also reinforce anxiety in the long run. The more someone avoids social situations, the harder it becomes to face them in the future, creating a cycle of isolation and distress. Living with social anxiety can be incredibly challenging. It can make it difficult to form and maintain friendships, pursue career opportunities, or enjoy everyday activities. The fear of being judged or rejected can hold individuals back from fully participating in social life, leading to feelings of loneliness and missed opportunities.

Understanding social anxiety and its impact is the first step toward finding ways to manage and overcome it. With the proper support, strategies, and treatment, individuals with social anxiety can learn to navigate social situations more confidently and reclaim their lives from the grips of fear and isolation.

The Amygdala:

It is a small, almond-shaped structure located deep within your brain. It's part of a more extensive network called the limbic system, which regulates emotions and memories. One of the Amygdala's main jobs is to process emotions, especially fear and anxiety.

In individuals with social anxiety, the Amygdala may be hyperactive, constantly perceiving social situations as threats and triggering a fear response. Imagine you have a tiny alarm system in your brain that goes off whenever it senses danger. Well, that's kind of what the Amygdala does. It's like a little bodyguard always on high alert and ready to jump into action.

Now, let's talk about social anxiety. In people with social anxiety, their Amygdala is like a super-sensitive alarm system. It's constantly scanning the environment for potential threats, and when it detects anything that could be seen as embarrassing or humiliating, it sets off alarm bells.

For example, let's say you're at a party and you accidentally spill your drink. Most people might feel embarrassed but can brush it off and move on. However, for someone with social anxiety, the Amygdala goes into overdrive. It interprets that simple mishap as a big red flag, signaling that everyone judges or laughs at them. This triggers a fear response, and suddenly their heart starts racing, their palms get sweaty, and they feel an overwhelming urge to escape.

This hyperactivity of the Amygdala in social anxiety is like having the volume turned up too high on your fear response. It constantly amplifies the perceived threats in social situations, making them seem far scarier than they actually are. It is as if your brain is always on high alert, ready to protect you from any potential embarrassment or rejection.

Understanding the role of the Amygdala in social anxiety is important because it helps explain why these fears can feel so intense and overwhelming. It's not just a matter of being shy or lacking confidence. **It's a biological response that's rooted in the brain's wiring.** By recognizing this, individuals with social anxiety can explore strategies and treatments that specifically target the Amygdala's hyperactivity, helping dial down the fear response and regain control over their social interactions.

Hyperactive Default Mode Network (DMN):

The Default Mode Network is a network of brain regions that activate when the mind is at rest or engaged in introspection. In individuals with social anxiety, the DMN may be overactive, leading to excessive self-focused thoughts, rumination, and negative self-evaluation in social situations. Imagine your brain as a bustling city with different regions constantly working together.

In people with social anxiety, this DMN neighborhood can sometimes become to active, almost like a burst of fireworks. Instead of giving your brain a break, it takes center stage, hogging all the attention. This increased activity can create a flood of self-focused thoughts that rush through your mind like a fast-paced train.

Just like when your mind goes on a self-reflection spree, this overactivity in the DMN can lead to endless thinking loops. It's like your brain is running a marathon of thoughts, constantly replaying past events or predicting future social interactions. This never-ending cycle of rumination can make you feel trapped, like a fly stuck in a web.

And it doesn't stop there. The DMN can also work hand in hand with its neighbor, the Negative Self-Evaluation Center. They team up to bombard you with a storm of negative thoughts and self-criticism. It's as if your brain has become a harsh judge, scrutinizing every move you make and magnifying any perceived flaws or mistakes.

This can make social situations feel like you're walking on eggshells, as your mind becomes preoccupied with self-doubt and worry. It's like wearing tinted glasses that make everything look distorted, painting a negative picture of yourself and the world around you.

Understanding how the DMN and social anxiety are connected can help shed light on what's happening in your brain. With this knowledge, **you can work on rewiring those connections, fostering positive self-talk, and building self-confidence.** You can step into the social world with a renewed sense of freedom and joy.

Negative Self-Evaluation Center:

This part of your brain focuses on criticizing and judging yourself. It's like having a really mean judge inside your head. This part of your brain plays a role in social anxiety and depression because it can make you feel like you're not good enough or that people are judging you negatively. It can also make you focus on your mistakes and flaws, making you feel bad about yourself. Understanding how this part of your brain works can help you work on building self-confidence and challenging negative thoughts about yourself.

Anxiety's Impact on Social Functioning and Depression:

Anxiety can lead to avoidance behavior, where individuals actively avoid social situations that trigger their anxiety. Avoidance behaviors may provide temporary relief but can ultimately perpetuate the cycle of fear and isolation. This avoidance can hinder the development and maintenance of meaningful social connections.

Cognitive Distortions:

Anxiety can influence how individuals interpret social situations, leading to cognitive distortions or negative thinking patterns. Common cognitive distortions include personalizing, where individuals blame themselves for negative interactions, and mind reading, assuming others' negative perceptions without evidence. These distortions can heighten feelings of depression and worsen social interactions.

Interpersonal Sensitivity:

Individuals with social anxiety often experience heightened interpersonal sensitivity, perceiving social cues and nonverbal communication as harmful or threatening. This hyper-awareness of others' judgments can fuel anxiety and make social interactions challenging and stressful.

The Social Brain:

It is a remarkable biological entity designed to navigate the intricate dynamics of human social interactions. However, this innate wiring can become a source of distress and anxious anticipation for individuals with social anxiety. Understanding the neurobiology behind social behavior and anxiety provides valuable insights into the challenges those with social anxiety face.

The interplay between mirror neurons, Oxytocin, and the Amygdala in the social brain highlights the complexity of human social interactions. Social anxiety disrupts this delicate balance, leading to avoidance behaviors, cognitive distortions, and heightened interpersonal sensitivity.

While depression and anxiety can both impact social connections negatively, the underlying mechanisms and behaviors associated with each condition differ. It is not uncommon for individuals to experience both depression and anxiety simultaneously, which can further complicate social interactions. Seeking professional help from a mental health practitioner can provide guidance and support in managing these challenges and improving overall social well-being.

Now let us take what we have learned in the preceding part of this chapter and put our newfound knowledge into practical applications in overcoming social isolation. You will explore evidence-based strategies and techniques to help individuals with social anxiety and depression overcome their fears, build confidence in social situations, and forge meaningful connections. By unveiling the mysteries of the social brain, we can empower individuals to navigate the social landscape with resilience, authenticity, and a sense of belonging.

The Science of Social Connections and How it Affects our Social Brain:

Humans are inherently social beings, wired to form and maintain connections with others. Understanding these biological foundations can help us appreciate how social relationships are crucial in managing anxiety. Individuals can build a supportive network that enhances their resilience and overall well-being by actively engaging in practical exercises centered around initiating and nurturing connections, utilizing technology, joining support groups, and fostering personal relationships.

Exercise: Reflect on a time when you felt supported and understood by someone close to you. Notice how that made you feel and how it affected your anxiety levels. Write down your observations.

"Tend and Befriend":

Evolutionary psychology suggests that social connections serve as a protective mechanism against depression. The concept of "tend and befriend" highlights the adaptive value of seeking support and forming social bonds during times of stress. By activating our social network, we can reduce anxiety levels and enhance our emotional well-being.

Exercise: Reach out to a friend or family member and share something you feel anxious about. Notice how their support and empathy can help alleviate your depression symptoms.

Exercise: Start by reaching out to one new person weekly through an online platform or a social event. Practice active listening and ask open-ended questions to foster meaningful conversations.

The Role of Neurotransmitters:

Several vital neurotransmitters, such as Oxytocin, dopamine, and serotonin, play a crucial role in social bonding and anxiety regulation. Oxytocin, known as the "love hormone," promotes feelings of trust and connectedness. Dopamine is associated with reward and motivation, while serotonin helps regulate mood and emotional stability. By understanding the influence of these neurotransmitters, we can explore strategies to enhance social connections and alleviate anxiety symptoms and depression.

Exercise: Engage in activities that promote the release of neurotransmitters, such as hugging a loved one, playing a game with friends, or participating in a group exercise class. Notice any changes in your mood and anxiety levels.

The Impact of Loneliness:

Social isolation and loneliness have been found to have detrimental effects on mental health, including increased anxiety. Loneliness triggers a stress response, leading to elevated cortisol levels and heightened depression. Recognizing the negative impact of loneliness underscores the importance of building and maintaining social connections as a means of anxiety prevention and depression management.

Exercise: Join a local club or community group that aligns with your interests. Attend a meeting or event to meet new people and foster potential social connections.

The Healing Power of Social Connections in Providing Emotional Support:

Social connections provide a platform for emotional support, empathy, and validation. Sharing our anxieties and fears with trusted individuals can help alleviate stress, foster a sense of belonging, and create a safe space for emotional expression.

Exercise: Set aside time to discuss your anxieties with a trusted friend or family member. Practice active listening and allow yourself to express your emotions. Even allow sadness or other negative emotions to surface. Every interaction you have doesn't have to be lighthearted. Allow whatever needs healing to naturally surface, making sure you're sharing in a safe and trusting environment.

Practical assistance is only one of the many benefits social connections can have; they also offer valuable benefits in managing anxiety. Whether helping with daily tasks, providing transportation, or offering guidance and advice. The tangible support from others can lighten the load and reduce depression. Role modeling, inspiration, and hearing stories of individuals who have successfully managed their anxiety through social connections can inspire hope and resilience. Witnessing others' experiences can provide guidance, validation, and motivation to seek and cultivate meaningful relationships.

Exercise: Identify a task or responsibility that is causing you anxiety. Seek the support of a friend, family member, or colleague to assist you with completing or managing that task.

Developing a Sense of Belonging:

Feeling a sense of belonging and acceptance within a community or social group is vital for mental well-being. Building strong social connections helps individuals create a support system that fosters resilience and buffers against stress. It promotes a positive sense of self, which enhances social connections and initiates nurturing friendships. Overcoming social anxiety is a crucial step in building new connections. Practical tips such as taking small steps, joining social activities or groups with shared interests, and practicing active listening and empathy help individuals feel more comfortable initiating conversations and cultivating friendships.

Exercise: Join a social or recreational group that shares your interests, such as a sports team or book club. Engage actively in group activities and conversations to foster a sense of belonging. **Use active listening with whoever you are with.** You will be amazed at how quickly you will bond with them.

Harnessing the Power of Technology:

Technology can be a valuable tool for fostering social connections, particularly for those who may find it challenging to engage in face-to-face interactions. Online communities, support groups, and social media platforms offer opportunities to connect with like-minded individuals, share experiences, and receive support.

Exercise: Join an online support group or community related to anxiety management or depression support. Participate in discussions, offer support, and seek advice from others who can relate to your experiences.

Joining Support Groups:

Seeking Out Specialized Anxiety and Depression Support Groups:

It can provide understanding, validation, and coping strategies for individuals who can relate to the challenges of managing anxiety. These groups offer a space to share experiences and learn from others' success stories. Engaging in social activities and exploring hobbies, clubs, and community events aligned with personal interests can provide opportunities for meeting new people and enhancing social connections. Participating in activities that bring joy and fulfillment helps reduce depression and build meaningful relationships.

Exercise: Research local support groups or seek online support groups dedicated to anxiety or depression management. Attend a meeting or join an online discussion to connect with individuals with similar experiences.

Engaging in Social Activities:

Participating in activities can enhance social connections. To engage in social activities, try this exercise:

Exercise: Explore local community event listings and select an event that interests you. Attend the event and try to strike up conversations with fellow attendees.

Volunteer Work:

Engaging in volunteering activities benefits the community and fosters social connections. By giving back, people can connect with like-minded people, develop a sense of purpose, and experience the positive effects of helping others.

When someone engages in volunteer work, they dedicate their time and skills to helping others in need without expecting anything in return. It's like being a superhero without a cape!

Volunteering is a win-win situation because not only does it benefit the community, but it also has a positive impact on the individuals who participate, **like planting seeds of kindness that grow and spread happiness.**

One of the fantastic things about volunteering is the opportunity to connect with people with similar interests and values. When you volunteer, **you often find yourself surrounded by like-minded individuals who are passionate** about making a difference. It's like joining a team where everyone works together towards a common goal, cheering each other on along the way.

By engaging in volunteer work, individuals also experience a sense of purpose. It's like finding a secret treasure that fills your heart with joy and fulfillment. You get to contribute to a cause you genuinely care about, knowing that your efforts are making a meaningful impact. Whether it's helping animals find forever homes, feeding the homeless, or tutoring children, the sense of purpose that comes from volunteer work can be incredibly empowering.

But the benefits of volunteering continue beyond there. When you help others selflessly, you also experience positive effects on your well-being. It's like a beautiful ripple effect that extends beyond the community. Volunteering has been shown to reduce stress, boost mood, and even improve physical health. It's like a magic potion that nourishes your soul and makes you happier and more fulfilled.

So, if you're considering volunteering, know it's about more than just giving your time and skills. It's about connecting with others, finding purpose, and experiencing the incredible power of helping others. It's a rewarding journey that will leave a lasting impact on both you and the community you support. When you volunteer, it's like stepping into a world where kindness and compassion are the superpowers that drive change. You transform into a real-life angel, swooping in to help those who most need it.

Imagine walking into a shelter for abandoned animals. The air is filled with the sound of wagging tails and grateful purrs. You can feel their warmth and happiness radiating through your fingertips as you spend time caring for these furry creatures. The love and gratitude they show make you realize just how impactful your actions are. Or picture yourself in a bustling soup kitchen. The smell of freshly cooked meals fills the air, mingling with the sounds of laughter and conversation. As you serve plates of warm food to those in need, you see their tired faces light up with gratitude. You get a glimpse into the lives of these individuals, understanding their struggles and finding fulfillment in knowing you are making a difference, even if it's just one meal at a time.

But the power of volunteering goes beyond your immediate impact on others. It extends to your own life as well. When you volunteer, you surround yourself with people who share your values. Picture a group united by a common cause, forming a tight-knit community. Together, you tackle challenges, offer support, and celebrate successes. This sense of belonging fills your heart with warmth and reminds you that you are not alone and can accomplish great things together.

As you dedicate your time and skills selflessly, you find a sense of empowering and fulfilling purpose. Imagine discovering a hidden magic world filled with joy and fulfillment. When you volunteer, that's precisely what you experience. You get to devote your energy to something you genuinely care about, knowing that every small action you take contributes to a more significant impact. Whether you're tutoring a struggling student, planting trees to protect the environment, or building homes for those in need, you know you are playing a vital role in creating a better world.

And the best part? Volunteering is not a one-way street. It's a beautiful exchange that benefits both the community and you, the volunteer. As you lovingly give your time, you receive incredible rewards in return. Picture a radiant smile on your face, a spring in your step, and a lightness in your heart. The stress melts away as you focus on the needs of others, leaving you feeling refreshed and rejuvenated. It's like a magic pill that boosts your mood, reduces stress, and even improves physical health.

So, if you're considering volunteering, take a leap of faith and embrace the profound impact it can have on your life. Immerse yourself in a world where kindness knows no bounds, where you can be a superhero to those in need. Your journey as a volunteer will leave a positive mark on the community you serve and bring immeasurable joy and fulfillment to your own life.

Exercise: Research local volunteer opportunities in your area. Select an organization or cause that resonates with you and dedicate a few hours each week or month to volunteer.

The Impact of Personal Relationships:

Family Bonds:

Family members can be a significant source of support in managing anxiety. Strengthening familial relationships, fostering open communication, and sharing responsibilities can alleviate anxiety symptoms and create a supportive environment.

Imagine a tightly-knit family where warmth and love flow freely between its members. In this supportive environment, family bonds have a unique power to ease anxiety. When families strengthen their relationships, a remarkable transformation takes place. It's as if they build a fortress of understanding and compassion, shielding each member from anxiety. They come together, creating a safe space where worries can be shared, emotions can be expressed, and burdens can be lightened. Open communication becomes the key that unlocks this fortress, allowing love and support to flow freely. Responsibilities are shared, distributing the weight of anxiety and creating a sense of unity. In this sanctuary, anxiety retreats, and a sense of security is restored.

Exercise: Plan regular family activities or meals where everyone can gather and spend quality time together. Engage in open and honest communication to foster a supportive family environment.

Romantic Relationships:

Secure and loving partnerships can provide a strong foundation for managing anxiety. The presence of a supportive partner who understands, empathizes, and actively participates in anxiety management can significantly reduce stress levels and foster resilience.

Imagine being in a romantic partnership where love and support are a solid foundation. In this loving embrace, anxiety loses its power over your emotions. A caring and understanding partner becomes a guiding light, illuminating the path toward anxiety management. They hold your hand, share your burdens, and walk beside you through the most challenging times. They listen without judgment, validate your feelings, and offer compassionate support. With their empathy and active involvement in anxiety management, Stress levels plummet. Together, you forge a powerful shield of resilience, facing anxiety head-on and emerging stronger than ever.

Exercise: Open a compassionate conversation with your partner about your anxiety. Identify ways to support each other and establish practices that promote a supportive partnership.

Workplace Connections:

Positive relationships in the workplace can reduce workplace stress and contribute to overall stress management. Cultivating healthy professional relationships, promoting supportive work environments, and fostering open communication can create a sense of security and reduce anxiety-related stressors.

Envision a workplace where positive relationships thrive like vibrant flowers in a flourishing garden. Workplace stress bends and breaks under the weight of genuine connections in this nurturing environment. Cultivating healthy professional relationships becomes the foundation of this supportive ecosystem. Colleagues provide technical assistance and emotional support, lifting each other up when stress threatens to take hold. Open communication channels flow freely, offering a lifeline to those grappling with anxiety-related stressors. This sense of security leaves anxiety with no room to grow, and a sense of calm and productivity prevails.

Exercise: Take the initiative to engage with your colleagues in a supportive and respectful manner. Schedule coffee breaks or team activities to foster a positive work environment.

Friendships and Peer Support:

Close friends can play a vital role in boosting resilience and providing emotional support. Nurturing existing friendships, engaging in quality time together, and being open to vulnerability and trust can deepen social connections and strengthen resilience against anxiety.

Picture a circle of close friends who gather with laughter and joy, forming a tight bond like a patchwork quilt of support. In this vibrant group, friendships become a powerful shield against anxiety. Friends hold the key to unlocking resilience and emotional support, offering a shoulder to lean on when anxiety feels overwhelming. Nurturing existing friendships becomes essential, weaving strands of trust and vulnerability. Spending quality time together, sharing experiences, and opening up about concerns creates a safe space to heal and grow. In this community, anxiety loses its hold as social connections deepen and resilience is fortified.

Exercise: Plan a social outing with a close friend, such as going for a walk, having a coffee date, or attending a local event. Prioritize active listening and open communication during your time together.

Exploring Online Relationships:

While online relationships can provide support and connection, it is essential to approach them with **caution**. Balancing digital connections with face-to-face interactions can help ensure a healthy social support network.

Consider the virtual world, a digital realm where connections are made at the touch of a button. While online relationships can offer support and moments of genuine connection, it's essential to approach them with awareness of online dangers. Picture a balancing act where digital connections and face-to-face interactions work in harmony. Online relationships can be like sparks of light, providing comfort and understanding. However, it's crucial to remember the irreplaceable value of physical interactions. Balancing screens with real-life connections ensures a healthy social support network, creating solid relationships that combat anxiety in the digital realm and the real world.

Exercise: Set boundaries for your online interactions, such as allocating a specific time for social media use. Prioritize face-to-face interactions and maintain meaningful connections with people offline.

In these personal relationships, anxiety is confronted with understanding, support, and resilience. Whether it's within the bonds of family, romance, workplace, friendships, or the exploration of online connections, the power of these relationships can transform anxiety into strength, creating a network of support that serves as a guiding light through life's challenges.

The Journey Towards Resilience:

Overcoming Challenges: Sharing personal anecdotes and success stories of individuals who transformed their depression through the power of social connections can inspire and provide hope for those on their own journey. Hearing how others **overcame challenges and built meaningful connections** can serve as motivation and encouragement. Embracing vulnerability and encouraging others to be open in seeking support, even in moments of difficulty, can help create deeper connections and foster empathy. Realizing that vulnerability is not a sign of weakness but an opportunity for growth and connection can empower your path and others in their journey toward managing depression.

Exercise: Seek out and read stories of individuals who have successfully overcome depression through social connections. Reflect on the challenges they faced and the strategies they used to overcome their depression.

Exercise: Identify a trusted friend, family member, or therapist and have a conversation where you share a vulnerable aspect of your depression. Practice being open and receptive to their support and guidance.

Seeking Professional Help:

Recognizing the importance of professional guidance is vital. Therapists, counselors, and other mental health professionals can provide specialized tools, techniques, and support to manage anxiety and cope with depression while helping individuals navigate and enhance their social connections.

Exercise: Research and schedule an appointment with a therapist or counselor who specializes in anxiety and depression management. Attend the session with an open mind and note any strategies or insights they provide.

Building Bridges to Joy and Resilience:

Individuals can build a supportive network that enhances their resilience and overall well-being by actively engaging in practical exercises centered around initiating and nurturing connections, utilizing technology, joining support groups, and fostering personal relationships. The journey toward managing anxiety becomes more hopeful and depression more manageable when practical strategies are applied to build bridges to joy and resilience.

The Power of Social Connections:

The power of social connections for managing anxiety is undeniable. Individuals can build a vibrant web of support and resilience by understanding the science behind social connections, embracing emotional support, nurturing existing relationships, and cultivating new connections. The journey toward depression management becomes more hopeful and empowering when we recognize the **healing potential of social connections.** By building bridges to joy and stability, we can navigate the challenges of anxiety and depression, finding solace, understanding, and strength in the company of others. Don't hesitate to **re-read each chapter,** having built your experience from previous chapters. With this knowledge, you will overcome anxiety and depression for long-term holistic health.

CITY GARDEN OF SOCIAL CONNECTIONS

SOFTLY ALLOW YOUR EYES to close and imagine a bustling city spread out before you. As you enter the city square, a radiant garden is laid before you. The air is alive with the sweet fragrance of blooming flowers, and the colors dance harmoniously, uplifting your spirits. The garden represents the variety of connections in your life, each flower symbolizing a different relationship or support system.

As you walk through the garden, you come across a majestic oak tree standing tall and strong. Its branches reach out, interconnecting with other trees, forming a network of support and stability. This tree represents your family, the roots that anchor you and provide a solid foundation. Each branch represents a different family member, their love and support branching out to embrace you. You can almost hear the whispers of their encouragement and feel the warmth of their love.

Continuing through the garden, you come across a sparkling fountain, its water cascading down in a graceful symphony. This fountain represents your close-knit friends, each droplet symbolizing a shared memory or laughter-filled moment. The water is playful and joyous, reflecting your deep connections and camaraderie with these cherished friends. As you dip your hands into the fountain, you feel a renewed sense of belonging and happiness, knowing you are surrounded by friends who bring light and laughter into your life.

Further along in the garden, you come across a delightful meadow filled with butterflies fluttering gracefully in the breeze. Each butterfly represents a connection you have within communities or interest groups. They flit from flower to flower, symbolizing the shared values and passions that bind you with others. As you watch the butterflies dance around you, you feel a profound sense of purpose and belonging, knowing you are part of a collective of like-minded individuals who understand and support your journey.

As you leave the meadow, a gentle rain begins to fall, each droplet representing acts of kindness and compassion you have both given and received. The rain showers the garden with love and nourishment, reminding you of the countless strangers who have shown you empathy and support in your darkest moments. You feel the warmth of gratitude wash over you, knowing that there is an abundance of kindness in the world, ready to lift you up and guide you through any challenges.

Finally, you come across a breathtaking rose garden, vibrant and filled with the aroma of love. Each rose represents a romantic connection, their petals opening to reveal the beauty and tenderness of these relationships. You are drawn to a particular rose, its color and fragrance reflecting the deep love and connection you share with someone special. As you caress the delicate petals, you feel the warmth of love embracing you, providing a sanctuary of safety and acceptance.

Standing at the heart of the garden, surrounded by the Love of Connections, you feel a profound sense of gratitude and strength. You understand that although anxiety and depression can be challenging, you are never alone. The garden reminds you that you are part of a vast, interconnected web of support and love. Each relationship and connection is like a unique flower, enriching your life and helping you bloom.

With this newfound awareness, you take a deep breath, absorbing this visualization's healing energy and vibrant imagery. You step forward, ready to embrace the Love of Connections in your life, knowing that you have a network of love and support to lift you up and guide you through any challenges that may arise. As you walk through life, you radiate the light, love, and strength you have absorbed from this metaphorical garden, spreading positivity and hope to others who may travel alongside you on your path.

CHAPTER SIXTEEN

RELAXATION THE ART OF BLISS

EMBRACE THE PLAYFUL SIDE OF RELAXATION IN CONQUERING ANXIETY AND DEPRESSION

Stress, anxiety, and depression are caused when we are living to please others. -Paulo Coelho

WELCOME TO THE ENCHANTING **world** of relaxation and leisure, where anxiety melts away and joy takes center stage over depression. In this chapter, we will venture beyond the conventional notions of relaxation and dive headfirst into fun and excitement. Explore a creative array of activities that will not only alleviate anxiety but also infuse depression with playfulness and delight. Get ready to unlock the transformative power of play and embrace relaxation methods that will have you **grinning from ear to ear.**

The Curious Connection of Fun, Depression Relief, and Vanishing Anxiety:

Prepare for a delightful surprise as we uncover how infusing relaxation and leisure with a touch of fun can provide profound relief from anxiety and depression:

1. **Neurochemical orchestra:** Fun-filled activities trigger a symphony of neurochemicals, including dopamine, oxytocin, and endorphins. These mood-enhancing chemicals generate feelings of pleasure, bonding, and overall well-being, effectively reducing depression.

2. **Distraction therapy:** Engaging in enjoyable and entertaining activities serves as a potent distraction from self-sabotaging thoughts. When you immerse yourself in the present moment, fully absorbed in a pleasurable endeavor, anxiety is gently pushed to the sidelines, and depression is benched, allowing you to get in the game of fun.

3. **Mindfulness in motion:** By embracing fun and exciting activities, you cultivate a state of mindfulness in motion. As you revel in the joyous experience, your attention is firmly anchored in the present, releasing worries about the past or future. This mindful immersion in play banishes anxiety, leaving room for spontaneity and enjoyment.

4. **Break the monotony:** Depression often thrives in the mundane and repetitive aspects of life. Injecting fun and excitement into your relaxation and leisure pursuits breaks the cycle of monotony, **rejuvenating your mind and spirit.** By diversifying your activities, you

create a vibrant array of experiences that nourish your soul and promote well-being.

5. Laughter as medicine: When was the last time you had a hearty laugh that made your sides ache and your cheeks hurt? Laughter is a potent antidote to depression, triggering the release of endorphins and reducing stress levels. Infusing relaxation into anxiety with **laughter lifts your spirits, lightens your heart,** and brings forth a sense of calm.

Enlivening Relaxation and Leisure Activities:

Say goodbye to dull and conventional relaxation techniques and embrace the vibrant world of fun and excitement. Engage in activities that not only relax but also ignite a spark of joy and creativity within you:

1. Playful Art Therapy: Rediscover your creative spirit through art-based activities that inspire joy and self-expression. Get your hands messy with finger painting, immerse yourself in a vibrant coloring book, or unleash your inner Picasso with vibrant and whimsical art projects. Allow your imagination to roam free as you explore new mediums and techniques, leaving any worrisome thoughts behind.

2. Dance Parties: Transform your living room into a discotheque and let loose your inner dancing diva. Blast your favorite tunes, unleash those dance moves, and giggle at your own rhythmically challenged steps. Dance with abandon, leaving anxiety in the dust and filling your soul with infectious joy. Your mood will be transformed for days.

3. Outdoor Adventure: Venture into the great outdoors and revel in the wonders of nature. Whether it's hiking through lush forests, kayaking down radiant rivers, or simply taking a leisurely stroll through a local park, immersing yourself in nature's beauty provides a serene escape from anxiety and a renewed sense of wonder. The beauty of nature is sure to lift your spirit.

4. Game Nights: Gather friends and family for a rollicking game night filled with laughter, competition, and good-natured fun. Engage in board games, card games, or even video games, letting go of worries and allowing the spirit of play to wash over you. Let the sound of shared laughter be an expression of depression-free living.

5. Comedy and Improv: Attend live comedy shows, watch humorous performances online, or try your hand at improv classes. **Laughter truly is the best medicine**, and comedy has a miraculous way of dissolving depression. Indulge in the entertaining realm of comedy, where anxiety is replaced by uproarious jubilant laughter.

Creating Space for Play and Fun:

Now that we've unveiled the power of playful relaxation, it's time to integrate these delightful activities into your daily life:

1. Prioritize playfulness: Make a conscious decision to prioritize play and fun in your life. Recognize the importance of leisure and relaxation in managing anxiety and commit to incorporating joyful activities regularly.

2. Step out of your comfort zone: Embrace the unfamiliar and embrace the unknown. Step out of your comfort zone and explore new activities that excite and inspire you. Indulge in the feeling of anticipation and the joy of discovery as you challenge yourself to try new things.

3. Make it a social affair: Engage in playful activities with friends, loved ones, or even like-minded strangers. The shared experience of joy and laughter amplifies the sense of fun and deepens connections, creating a support system of laughter and camaraderie.

4. Incorporate humor into your daily life: Seek out humor in everyday situations, surround yourself with comedic books, movies, and shows, and cultivate humorous perspectives. Infusing humor into your life not only reduces depression but also shifts your mindset, enabling you to face challenges with a lighter heart.

5. Celebrate small moments of joy: Acknowledge and savor the small moments of joy and happiness that arise throughout your day. Whether it's enjoying a delicious meal, dancing spontaneously, or engaging in a light-hearted conversation, cherish these moments as reminders of the power of play and delight.

In this chapter, we have tapped into the transformative power of play and discovered how infusing relaxation and leisure with fun can dismantle anxiety's grip on our lives. With a playful approach to relaxation, we unlock neurochemical wonders, distract the mind from depressive thoughts, and cultivate a state of mindfulness in motion. We invite laughter, joy, and fulfillment into our lives. So, dance with abandon, create vibrant art, immerse yourself in nature, and revel in the delights of game nights and comedy shows. Say "**yes**" to **playful relaxation** and discover a life free from anxiety or depression.

Relaxing on a Cloud

Clouds come floating into my life, no longer to carry rain or usher storm, but to add color to my sunset sky.-Thich Nhat Hanh

A s YOU SIT IN a state of ease and relaxation, close your eyes and imagine the sky above you. Visualize a sun-drenched canvas stretching out endlessly, adorned with fluffy, billowing clouds of various shapes and sizes. The gentle sway of the clouds reflects the rhythm of your breath, symbolizing the ebb and flow of peace and tranquility within you.

With each breath in, visualize the pure, rejuvenating energy of the sky infusing your body and mind. As you exhale, release any tension or worries, allowing them to dissolve into the vast expanse of the atmosphere. Watch as these concerns transform into delicate wisps of vapor, gently carried away by the breezes of tranquility.

As you continue to breathe deeply, imagine yourself enveloped by the soft embrace of a cloud: this ethereal mass supports and cradles you, cocooning you in a comforting blanket of relaxation. Feel your body floating weightlessly, as though you are effortlessly drifting among the clouds.

The cloud beneath you cradles your body, molding to your form and providing a soothing, cloud-like cushion. Allow yourself to surrender to this gentle support, releasing any tension or resistance held within. Feel your muscles relax, and your body melts into the plushness of the cloud.

As you bask in the serenity of this cloud sanctuary, observe the ever-changing shapes and patterns of the clouds above. Like a vibrant choreography, they dance gracefully across the deep-blue sky, carrying with them a sense of lightness and freedom. Each shape that forms and dissipates symbolizes the impermanence of thoughts and worries, reminding you to let them pass with ease.

Notice how the soft, cool touch of the cloud against your skin brings a profound sense of refreshment and rejuvenation. Let the cloud's gentle embrace soothe any physical discomfort or tension, creating a space of deep relaxation within your body.

As you surrender to the peaceful ambiance of the clouds, allow your mind to wander and daydream. Explore the limitless expanse of your imagination, inspired by the whimsical forms and colors painted across the sky. Let your thoughts and creative energy soar, unrestricted by the boundaries of daily life.

In this tranquil haven, time becomes an abstract concept as the clouds effortlessly carry you into a state of timelessness. Thoughts and worries fade into insignificance while a profound sense of peace and clarity washes over your being. Allow yourself to simply be merging with the essence of the clouds and experiencing a profound connection to the expansive beauty of the world.

As you continue to visualize the serene sky above, the warm rays of the sun gently caress your skin, filling you with a sense of peace and renewal. The vibrant hues of the sky paint a masterpiece of tranquility, inviting you to immerse yourself in the beauty of the moment. With each inhale, feel the energy of the sun infusing your being with vitality and warmth, awakening every cell in your body to the radiance of the present moment.

As you exhale, release any lingering doubts or fears that may cloud your mind, allowing them to dissolve into the vast expanse of the heavens. As the wind carries these worries away, feel a lightness in your heart and mind, liberated from the burdens that once weighed you down. The gentle rustle of the breeze whispers words of encouragement, reminding you of your inherent strength and resilience.

In this state of blissful serenity, let your imagination soar as freely as the birds that glide effortlessly through the sky. Embrace the boundless possibilities that lie before you, inspired by the vast expanse of the horizon stretching endlessly before you. Allow your dreams to take flight, guided by the winds of passion and purpose, as you navigate the uncharted territories of your inner landscape.

The ever-changing canvas of the sky mirrors the ebb and flow of life's rhythms, a reminder that change is inevitable and growth is constant. Embrace the transient nature of existence, finding solace in the knowledge that every storm eventually gives way to clear skies and new beginnings. With each passing cloud, witness the beauty of impermanence, allowing it to instill in you a sense of gratitude for the fleeting moments of joy and sorrow that shape your journey.

As you bring your awareness back to the present moment, carry with you the peace and clarity you found among the clouds. Let the memory of this tranquil sanctuary guide you in times of uncertainty and unrest, serving as a beacon of hope and light in the darkest of nights. Embrace the infinite possibilities that lie within you, knowing that you possess the strength and wisdom to overcome any storm and emerge stronger and more resilient than before.

With a renewed sense of peace and purpose, open your eyes to the world around you, ready to face each new day with courage and grace. May the beauty of the sky's embrace forever remind you of the boundless potential that resides within you, waiting to be unleashed and shared with the world. When you are ready to return, gradually bring your awareness back to your physical body. Feel the sensation of your breath and the weight of your body resting on the surface below. Carry with you the tranquility and rejuvenation you found among the clouds, allowing it to infuse your everyday life, bringing a sense of calm and blissful harmony.

As you open your eyes, may the memory of the cloud's embrace remind you to always seek moments of relaxation and serenity, allowing your inner sky to be forever adorned with the beauty and tranquility of clouds.

Embracing the journey:

As we reach the end of this transformative journey through anxiety, we are reminded of the incredible power that resides within each and every one of us. We have explored the depths of depression's fears, doubts, and uncertainties, but we have also **discovered the boundless strength and resilience that lies dormant within our souls**. Now, armed with the knowledge and tools we have gained, let us step forward into the world with renewed courage and unrestrained compassion.

Anxiety, once an unwelcome guest, has transformed into a formidable teacher, offering us invaluable lessons along the way. It has shown us the importance of self-compassion, **teaching us to embrace our imperfections and love ourselves unconditionally.** Through the darkest moments of depression, we have learned to extend a gentle hand and say, **"I am enough, just as I am."**

Our journey has also illuminated the significance of the mind-body connection. We have delved deep into the practice of mindfulness, nurturing the present moment and cultivating a sense of inner calm. In these moments of awareness, we have discovered that depression is not an enemy to be conquered but rather a **welcomed invitation to explore ourselves more fully. Through mindfulness,** we have discovered that anxiety is not who we are but merely a passing visitor in the landscape of our lives.

The power of community and human connection has played a significant role in our journey. We have come to realize that we are not alone in our struggles, as countless others have walked a similar path. Through open and honest conversations, we have found solace and support, creating a network of strength and understanding. **Together, we have shattered the barriers of isolation.**

EPILOGUE

VICTORIA'S ODYSSEY

ONCE UPON A TIME, in the charming town of Willowbrook, nestled in the picturesque rolling hills of the countryside, lived a young woman named Victoria. With her fiery red hair and sparkling green eyes, Victoria radiated an infectious energy that drew people toward her. She had an unwavering, determined spirit and a heart brimming with dreams and aspirations.

But beneath Victoria's vibrant exterior lay a relentless battle that threatened to overshadow her every step. Anxiety, a formidable foe, had woven its way into the very fabric of her being. Like an invisible serpent, it coiled around her thoughts, injecting poison into her mind and casting suffocating darkness over her every endeavor.

Though Victoria yearned to seize the opportunities that beckoned her, her anxiety clung to her like a relentless shadow. It whispered insidious doubts in her ear, reminding her of how she could fail. It crafted intricate webs of negative thoughts, trapping her in a self-imposed cage of fear, preventing her from embracing the vibrant magnificence of life.

But in the deep recesses of her heart, a fierce spirit stirred. Victoria refused to be defined by her anxiety any longer. She solemnly vowed to confront her fears head-on, break free from the chains that bound her, and reclaim her life in all its resplendent glory.

And so, armed with an unwavering determination, Victoria embarked on a transformative journey of self-discovery and healing. With each brave step, she pushed herself beyond the confines of her comfort zone, gradually expanding her horizons and embracing the unknown.

Recognizing that she couldn't navigate this path alone, Victoria sought solace in the gentle guidance of a compassionate counselor named Dr. Harper. Together, they ventured into the depths of her anxiety, unraveling its tangled roots and discovering the power within her to overcome its suffocating grip.

With Dr. Harper's guidance, Victoria discovered the power of mindfulness and learned to tame her racing thoughts. She found sanctuary in the present moment through practiced breathwork, allowing herself to ground and regain control when anxiety threatened to overwhelm her.

Yet, therapy alone was not enough for Victoria. Drawing inspiration from the vast wonders of the natural world, she sought solace in the healing embrace of Mother Nature. She traversed verdant trails, where the caress of the wind and birdsong became her companions. Amongst towering trees and babbling brooks, Victoria found solace amidst the symphony of nature, whispering secrets of resilience and strength into her soul.

But perhaps the most invaluable treasure she found on her journey was a community of kindred spirits. Victoria connected with others who had waged their own battles against anxiety. They formed a tribe of warriors bound by shared experiences and an unyielding determination to overcome their fears. They found strength and solace in each other's unwavering support, encouraging one another to face their anxieties head-on.

As months ebbed into years, Victoria discovered that her anxiety, once a fierce storm, was now a gentle breeze that drifted through her life. She mastered the art of challenging negative thoughts, plucking them like weeds from the depths of her mind, and replacing them with empowering affirmations.

One fateful day, Victoria found herself in an awe-inspiring moment. Standing before a packed auditorium, she was poised to deliver a speech she had painstakingly crafted. Her heart thrummed with a renewed vitality, her palms moistened with anticipation. But instead of allowing her anxiety to consume her, she summoned her inner warrior, envisioning herself as a majestic phoenix, ready to rise from the ashes.

Her voice resonated with passion and authenticity with each word she spoke, unleashing a kaleidoscope of emotions within her audience. Every intonation carried the weight of her triumph, inspiring others to embrace their vulnerabilities and reclaim their lives. The following applause was a symphony of validation, a testament to the power of one person's courage to ignite change.

From that moment on, Victoria's life blossomed and transformed into vibrant colors of endless possibilities. She fearlessly pursued opportunities, trampling over her fears with unbridled determination. She ventured into distant lands, her adventurous spirit soaring to new heights. A touch of serendipity graced her path, leading her to forge deep connections with kindred souls, savoring every moment of shared laughter and shared longing.

Victoria's story bloomed as an everlasting testament to the resilience of the human spirit. She inspired countless others through her journey of conquering anxiety, implanting the seed of hope within their hearts. And as the years glided by, Victoria held fast to the battles she fought, ever grateful for the person she had become, forever thankful for her journey of triumph over anxiety.

As we move forward, let us remember that anxiety does not define us. Instead, it is an opportunity for growth and empowerment. We have discovered the transformative potential within our minds, hearts, and souls, and now we carry that light out into the world. We have the power to make a difference, not only in our own lives but also in the lives of others.

Let us stand tall, the embodiment of resilience and compassion, and share our stories with courage and vulnerability. By speaking our truths, we inspire others to find their own strength and face their anxieties head-on. Together, we can create a world where stress and depression are met with understanding and kindness and each individual feels seen and accepted.

So, my fellow travelers, as we bid farewell to the pages of this book, let us embrace the unknown with open arms. We have navigated the labyrinth of negative emotions and emerged on the other side, transformed in countless ways. Continue to honor your progress, practice self-care, and never lose sight of your inherent worth.

May your journey be filled with love, joy, and infinite possibilities. May you step boldly into the world, knowing that you are equipped with the tools to conquer any challenge that comes your way. May your heart always be filled with unwavering courage and boundless compassion.

Remember, dear reader, the power lies within YOU. Embrace it, cherish it, and let it guide you on the Beautiful Journey Called Life.

With Love and Gratitude

I leave you with this loving-kindness meditation to savor and take with you wherever you may happily wander. If this book has made a difference in your journey with anxiety and depression, **Please leave a review on Amazon below. https://amzn.to/43YX0cU**

Scan me

https://amzn.to/43YX0cU

The light within me salutes the light within you!

Loving Kindness Meditation

May all beings be happy. May all beings be safe.
May all beings be healthy. May all beings live with
ease. -The Metta Sutta

As you settle into your quiet and peaceful space, take a moment to fully immerse yourself in the present moment. Feel the support of the chair or cushion beneath you, grounding your body and allowing you to relax. Close your eyes and begin to turn your attention inward, tuning into the sensations of your breath.

With each inhale, feel the cool air entering your nostrils and filling your lungs. Picture this breath as a cleansing wave of love and compassion, washing away any tension or resistance in your body and mind. As you exhale, imagine warm exhalations carrying away any negative or stagnant energy, making room for the presence of love and kindness.

Now, shift your focus to your heart center, the area in the center of your chest where emotions are felt. Visualize a radiant light at this center, glowing with a soft and warm hue. This light represents the love and compassion that resides within you, a boundless wellspring that is always available to you.

With each breath in, allow this light to expand and fill your entire body, permeating every cell and fiber. Feel the warmth and comfort that this light brings, soothing any tension or discomfort that may be present. As your body relaxes further, let this light spread beyond your physical being, extending outwards and enveloping your entire being in a bubble of loving-kindness.

Now, as you repeat heartfelt phrases to yourself, let the words flow from the depths of your heart. Imagine these words resonating with the very core of your being. Say to yourself, "May I be safe and at ease. May I be happy and healthy." Allow the meaning and intention of these phrases to sink in, filling you with a sense of love and care.

As you continue to breathe deeply, gradually extend these wishes to your loved ones, friends, and acquaintances. Visualize each person, one by one, and send them your loving kindness. Imagine them filled with joy, peace, and well-being. Picture their faces lighting up with smiles and their hearts being uplifted as they receive your loving kindness. Say, "May they be safe and at ease. May they be happy and healthy."

Now, expand your loving-kindness even further. Imagine your wishes for love and compassion encompassing all beings across the universe. Visualize a wave of loving-kindness emanating from your heart and spreading outwards, touching every being it encounters.

Whether human or animal, known or unknown, let your love and compassion be boundless and inclusive. Feel a deep sense of inter-connectedness as you realize that we are all part of this vast web of existence.

As you gradually conclude the meditation, take a moment to honor and appreciate the love and kindness you have cultivated within yourself and shared with others. Feel the warmth and gentle energy of your heart center, knowing the power and impact it holds. Carry this love and compassion with you as you go about your day, allow-ing it to guide your actions and interactions. Remember that you have made a positive contribution to the world simply by cultivating love and kindness within yourself.

Loving-Kindness Meditation can be practiced for as long as you like, whether it's a few minutes or a longer duration. The key is to approach it with intention and an open heart, allowing yourself to be fully present and receptive to the boundless love and kindness that reside within you. Embrace this practice as a way to nourish your own well-being and strengthen the bonds of love and con-nection with all beings.

Carry out a random act of kindness, with no expectation of reward, safe in the knowledge that one day someone might do the same for you. -Princess Diana

REFERENCES

Ben-Menachem, E.(2001) Vagus nerve stimulation, side effects, and long-term safety. Journal of Clinical Neurophysiology, 18(5), 415-418

Cameron, M. E. (2014). Yoga. In R. Lindquist, M. Snyder, & M. F. Tracy (Eds.), Complementary and alternative therapies in nursing (7th ed., pp. 139–152). Springer Publishing Company.

Ciarrochi, J., Hayes, L. L., & Hall, K. (. (2020). Your life, your way: skills to help teens manage emotions and build resilience. Oakland, CA, Instant Help Books, an imprint of New Harbinger Publications, Inc.

Feinstein, D. (2023). Integrating the manual stimulation of acupuncture points into psychotherapy: A systematic review with clinical recommendations. Journal of Psychotherapy Integration, 33(1), 47–67.

Field, T. (2009). Aromatherapy. In T. Field, Complementary and alternative therapies research (pp. 89–96). American Psychological Association.

Hay, L. L. (1999). You can heal your life. Carlsbad, CA, Hay House.

Kipling, R. (1994). Kim (C. Watts, Ed.). Wordsworth Editions.

Nhất Hạnh., & Kotler, A. (1992). Peace is every step: the path of mindfulness in everyday life. Bantam trade paperback edition. New York, Bantam Books.

Peck, M. S. 1. (1978). The road less traveled: a new psychology of love, traditional values, and spiritual growth. New York, Simon and Schuster.

Positive Daily Affirmations: Is There Science Behind It? 4 Mar 2019 by Catherine Moore, Psychologist, MBA Scientifically reviewed by Jo Nash, Ph.D.

Simmons, S. (2012). I'm your man: the life of Leonard Cohen. New York, Ecco Press/HarperCollins Publishers.

Ram Dass., & Das, R. (2010). Be love now: the path of the heart. New York, HarperOne.

Xiv, D. L., & Cutler, H. C. (1999). The art of happiness. Hodder Paperback.

ABOUT THE AUTHOR

LILLYN LOVE

From Kathmandu to Kodiak, I felt like I was
dragging a ball and chain of Anxiety and
Depression until I found these life- changing
solutions.
Please!
Join me on your journey and change your life too!

L ILLY WAS FEATURED FRONT page in the New York Times Sunday
Magazine (What Does a Parrot Know About PTSD Charles Siebert)
for her groundbreaking work with Dr. Lorin Lindner at Serenity Park,
established at the West Los Angeles Veterans Administration. She worked
daily with veterans suffering from severe PTSD and trauma in a natural

setting bonding rescue parrots with veterans in a therapeutic approach with great success for both parrots and veterans. Lilly simply states, "if you follow this guide, you're going to feel better and find more happiness." She believes in a holistic approach to healing mind, body, and spirit. She lives on her sailboat in Mexico where she writes and creates her mesmerizing illustrations that please the eye and tickle the subconscious. Catch her blog: ***The Realistic Holistic; Living Holistically Realistically*** at https://lillovepublishing.com.

Lillys spiritual path started as a Coast Guard Helicopter Rescue crewmember in Alaska after which she systematically searched to find harmony in a variety of disciplines from massage therapy to hypnotherapy and meditation adding Cognitive-Behavioral Therapies where she managed Serenity Park a therapy program at the West Los Angeles Veterans Administration.

www.ingramcontent.com/pod-product-compliance
Lightning Source LLC
Chambersburg PA
CBHW020437130626
46549CB00001B/185

9 798989 236206